T0194483

# Dear
# SURVIVOR

## LET'S TALK

AUDREY J. ELLIS

WESTBOW
PRESS®
A DIVISION OF THOMAS NELSON
& ZONDERVAN

WestBow Press books may be ordered through booksellers or by contacting:

WestBow Press
A Division of Thomas Nelson & Zondervan
1663 Liberty Drive
Bloomington, IN 47403
www.westbowpress.com
1 (866) 928-1240

Because of the dynamic nature of the Internet, any web addresses or links contained in this book may have changed since publication and may no longer be valid. The views expressed in this work are solely those of the author and do not necessarily reflect the views of the publisher, and the publisher hereby disclaims any responsibility for them.

This book is a work of non-fiction. Unless otherwise noted, the author and the publisher make no explicit guarantees as to the accuracy of the information contained in this book and in some cases, names of people and places have been altered to protect their privacy.

Any people depicted in stock imagery provided by Getty Images are models, and such images are being used for illustrative purposes only. Certain stock imagery © Getty Images.

Scripture taken from the New King James Version®. Copyright © 1982 by Thomas Nelson. Used by permission. All rights reserved.

Scripture quotations marked (AMP) are taken from the Amplified Bible, Copyright © 1954, 1958, 1962, 1964, 1965, 1987 by The Lockman Foundation. Used by permission.

Scripture quotations marked (NLT) are taken from the Holy Bible, New Living Translation, copyright © 1996, 2004, 2007 by Tyndale House Foundation. Used by permission of Tyndale House Publishers, Inc., Carol Stream, Illinois 60188. All rights reserved.

ISBN: 978-1-9736-2545-2 (sc)
ISBN: 978-1-9736-2544-5 (hc)
ISBN: 978-1-9736-2546-9 (e)

Library of Congress Control Number: 2018904304

Print information available on the last page.

WestBow Press rev. date: 04/19/2018

# CONTENTS

Preface ................................................................vii
Acknowledgments .................................................xi
I Still Win................................................................ xiii

Chapter 1. Dear Survivor:  Why Not You?............................ 1
Chapter 2. Dear Survivor:  Do Not Try to Figure It Out! .... 9
Chapter 3. Dear Survivor:  What Do You Have to
                                            Say about This? ......................... 17
Chapter 4. Dear Survivor:  Stop and Focus!.........................27
Chapter 5. Dear Survivor:  I'm Sorry for Your Loss.............35
Chapter 6. Dear Survivor:  They Really Don't Know
                                            What to Say...............................43
Chapter 7. Dear Survivor:  It's Okay to Not Be Okay.........50
Chapter 8. Dear Survivor:  God Hears and Sees You..........59
Chapter 9. Dear Survivor:  Look Up and Get Up!...............66
Chapter 10. Dear Survivor: Good Is Coming.......................74
Chapter 11. Dear Survivor: It's a Process:
                                            Think about Living...................81
Chapter 12. Dear Survivor: Consider What He Has
                                            Done and Then Tell Someone...88
Final Word.  Jesus Is the Cure! .............................................97

Notes.........................................................................99

# PREFACE

Dear Survivor,

I am a breast cancer survivor. I am not suggesting that you must share my story, but I am sure that you have your own unique story of survival. Now, you may be thinking, *I'm not a survivor. I just received the dreadful news. I'm not there yet.* While there are no traces of cancer in my body and my treatments are complete, have I survived cancer? I choose to believe that the answer is yes. I will not allow my mind to become enslaved with doubt or fear of cancer's return.

Cancer was hard for me to say after it became part of my medical history. Surviving was the opposite of dying. Because you are able to read this, you are alive. You are a survivor.

I am writing to you because I refused to talk to other cancer patients, who had shared my experience as their own, even though I had a lot of questions. I wanted answers but not conversations about cancer.

In the beginning, each time someone referred me to other *survivors* of cancer, I never made contact with them. It wasn't that I didn't value their journey but that I did not want to talk about the "c" word. I became overwhelmed with questions: What will I say? How can this help me? Why would I subject myself to such a vulnerable place of expression? Will my fear show? Will my weaknesses show? What will their experiences do for me?

While the questions rolled in, my willingness to reach out to other survivors was nonexistent.

Just in case you don't want to talk to anyone either, I am writing to you about my experience of how God healed me and received all the glory for it! It's not as personal as a face to face conversation, but it is a personal account of how God gave me strength, wisdom, and peace during a time when it felt like my life had been turned upside down, inside out, and rolled down a hill.

We don't have to make eye contact, have coffee, or get dressed up for this conversation. I would love it if your mind would become refocused on living by the last page. You are still here. You survived the bad news. Maybe there has not been any bad news, but you are preparing yourself for any such battles that might come your way. You still have breath to praise God for all the small victories.

While there are no absolute truths in the scientific world of cancer research (at least this is my opinion), let me assure you there are absolute truths in God's Word and His ability to heal you and give you eternal life. You have nothing to lose and you have the story of how one woman fought the battle against cancer to gain.

I can say cancer now and trust me; you will eventually be able to do so too. You will say it loud and clear when you feel it is time to take back your power from the dreadful disease or whatever situation has put you into survival mode.

I promise not to tell anyone what we discuss—that your eyes are red from crying or what you may jot down on the side of a paragraph that reaches your pain. You can consider me your pen pal. Depending on your age, you may remember the adventure of writing to a stranger who lived in a place you may have never visited. On the contrary, you and I will be pen pals who share an adventure from the same place in life. The adventure is fighting for our lives, and the place is pain. Oh, but it gets better.

I only ask you for one thing in return. After reading my testimony, or what I refer to as my story, I challenge you to tell everyone you know about how God healed you. You may feel that you are not there yet either. As time moves on and your faith increases, you will get there and desire to shout your story from the mountaintops.

I believe that I was healed before the treatments even began. I am confident that this book is a part of my purpose, my living, and my giving back for all God has done for me. As we explore my journey battling cancer, it will not be exactly like your story nor will your journey be like the next person's. Yet the same God will provide you with the same results—healing and eternal life.

I am now able to share my story because my feet have been planted on the foundation of my testimony, as it is written, "I shall not die, but live, and declare the works of the Lord" (Psalm 118:17). It isn't about anything fascinating that I did or that I came up with a cure but that I relied on the source that is the cure. Again, I know you don't want to be so personal with a stranger at this moment. Let's move forward so that I may share my story with you and allow you to know me better.

It was the power of God's Word that healed me. I experienced healing power as I spoke His word over my body. God speaks to Jeremiah: "'Is not My word like a fire?' says the Lord, 'and like a hammer that breaks the rocks in pieces?'" (Jeremiah 23:29). God's Word will consume unpleasant circumstances like a fire and break them into pieces. Therefore, speak God's Word, to set sickness, turmoil, and every problem on fire and beat them into pieces. At the end of each chapter I have a "Burn and Break" section with selected scriptures and a prayer that I have written to share with you. The Bible verses at the end of each chapter are those that were essential to me. Your own personal search of scripture for additional daily meditation verses is ideal.

P.S. I forgot to mention that it was no accident that you decided to pick up this book, whether it was a gift, accidental purchase, or something you found lying in a parking lot. God had you in mind when I began the manuscript. He is concerned about you, right now, today, and in this moment, and wants you to begin living!

Sincerely,
Your sister in survival

# ACKNOWLEDGMENTS

To my husband, Dayle: I thank you for loving me unconditionally and for believing in my dreams (sometimes more than I believe). I love you forever. No white horse but you are wearing armor.

To my sons Ryan and Devin: May the Lord bless you as you become courageous and confident men of God.

To Momma and Daddy: Thank you both for giving me one of the greatest gifts of life—the value of hard work.

To Diana Williams: Thank you, Sis, for being a reader and for your encouragement during this writing journey.

To Melissa Mims and Ralph Slayton: You both were angels sent from God as I entered the Wounded Warrior Detachment, Bethesda, Maryland. The assurance that I saw in your faces had me convinced that I was just checking into another temporary duty station.

To my Grace Church, VA family: Finding Grace was God's plan that has continued to nurture my soul.

# I STILL WIN

Cancer,

Your name is hard to pronounce since it's attached to my name.
I never had problems saying it before, but now I pause before
I proclaim.

The possibilities were slim and the chances were few.
"How did you find me?" is the question I wish I knew the
answer to.

You came from dark moments, silently during the stress,
As I went about my life doing my very best.

How dare you interrupt the course of my life,
Causing my family separation and so much strife.

Your attempt to destroy me has been aborted and will not
succeed,
As I have called on my Creator during this time of need.

He said He would never forsake me, and I believe that He is
near.
He told me that He has given me power, not a spirit of fear.

The miracles He worked in the days of old

Are more than just parables that were told.

He is unchangeable, and His willingness to heal is still the same.
It is up to me. Only if I have no faith can you remain.

Your name is deceiving, and I refuse to give in.
I discovered you early, so the bottom line is *I win!*

# CHAPTER 1

# Why Not You?

### My Story

## October 31, 2012

Father God, although it appears that I am going around and around a very familiar mountain as I deal with the multiple cysts that have been found in my breast, I know that You are able. The test results will be back sooner than they initially stated—now that's good news.

God, increase my faith. I know you are a healer, and this should be a very simple process for me, but I almost began to feel sorry for myself, and that is never good. I thank you for Dayle, my soul sistahs, and my family members, who wouldn't let me stay down too long. God, I look forward to rejoicing in victory when the test results come back.

✿✿✿

1

> At Joppa there was a certain disciple named Tabitha, which is translated Dorcas. This woman was full of good works and charitable deeds which she did. (Acts 9:36)

In Acts 9, a woman of great character becomes sick and dies. She was described as a believer and as someone who was full of good works and charitable deeds. I am still a student of the Bible, but without doubt, I believe that if the Bible refers to someone as "good," there is no compromise in that person's character. The Bible teaches all about being good, doing good, and living good—guess that's why it is also known as the Good Book!

**Wondering why it happened is like searching for a small pearl on a sandy beach.**

Dorcas makes her debut in the pages of the greatest piece of literature ever written in the history of the earth, which was inspired by God. The way she lived was in the writer's foremost thoughts and immediately followed her name. It is not by chance that we meet her; it is on purpose and with a life lesson. Her example is something that we, as believers, need to know. Her age and complete bio are not listed. All that we need is written in verses 36–42. The story of her life is a gift of words from God. What does God intend for us to learn from it?

## The Big Question

*Why me?* flashed boldly in large neon letters across the big screen of my thoughts. What had I done so wrong that I deserved another all-expense-paid trip to the forsaken land of cancer? I was a good person, was nice to *most* people, and served the Lord in church. As a licensed minister of His gospel, I would tell people of His goodness. Oh, how I proclaimed He was a healer because He had healed me in 2005 and 2009. The question tried to consume me, but I had to let it go.

I now realize that this question is not strange or a sign of faithlessness. In a world where actions equal consequences, it is quite normal to contemplate the reason behind your illness, pain, chaos, or suffering. Allowing these thoughts to linger is like purposely placing a boulder on your roof and expecting it to roll off instead of crashing through. Searching God's Word for your answers will lead you to much needed comfort and cause the big question to lose its power and immensity.

Dorcas's survival story does not state that she asked, "Why me?" But her character description made me ask the question for her. Why would she have to suffer sickness and an untimely death?

In His infinite wisdom, God knew this story would provide clarity—although bad things happen to good people, it is all for His glory. Afflictions are sure to come upon us as believers, but the psalmist records in Psalm 34:19 that God will deliver us from them all. To our knowledge, Dorcas did not complain, but what about her circle of friends?

## Your Circle Is Important

Dorcas had a crew of people who saw her dead body but believed it could be healed and restored. Her crew took action. They pursued a remedy that had already been witnessed in their land—the Holy Spirit moving through Peter. Jesus had declared that His disciples would be able to do great works (see John 14:12). Peter had received healing power by the Holy Spirit and had performed many signs and wonders. Her crew went with urgency and asked that Peter come and not delay.

Who is in your circle? When you shared your situation with them, what did they do? Did they run away? People are not always able to handle the pressure and stress of another person's struggles. Did they tell you that they were going to stay by your side until the end—you know, "ride or die"? I thank God for my faithful husband and friends. They chose to stand by my side and to take action through much fasting and prayer to God, our Healer.

## Works Alone Do Not Save

Long ago, widows were shown honor, and doing right by them was important (see 1 Timothy 5:3–16). The widows came forth with tunics (garments) that Dorcas had made for them while she had been alive (see Acts 9:39). When Peter arrived, he found the widows weeping over Dorcas's dead body. They tried desperately to tell him all that she had done for them. We can only imagine the sound of the weeping and of everyone speaking at once.

Peter's response, while somewhat shocking, suggests that he did not deem it necessary to hear of every good deed Dorcas had performed or the good works she had sown into the lives of the widows. This clearly shows that his ability to heal her was not dependent on her works and deeds. In fact, if he had used her works as his motivation, he would have carefully listened to each story and observed the tangible works of her hands. Instead, Peter sent the widows out of the room, humbled himself, prayed, and then commanded Dorcas to rise.

Your works will not save you from the death of your body or your circumstances. Only the power of God can bring what has died back from its state of decay. Our works cannot be confused with our right for blessings and healing.

Consequently, our works are not to be discounted. The Bible says, "For God will bring every work into judgment, including every secret thing, whether good or evil" (Ecclesiastes 12:14). At the appointed time, they will be judged by God. Matthew 5:16 tells us, "Let your light shine before men in such a way that they may see your good deeds and moral excellence, and [recognize and honor and] glorify your Father who is in Heaven" (AMP).

## Continuing in Good Works Is Important

Please do not decide that if your works cannot keep you from experiencing tragedy then you may as well do whatever you want. No, that is definitely not my message. The works that you do are profitable to you and everyone around you. The Bible tells us, "This is a faithful saying, and these things I want you to affirm constantly, that those who have believed in God should be careful to maintain good works. These things are good and profitable to men" (Titus 3:8).

It is good to do good and to be good to people. Paul, the author of Titus, instructs, "And let our people also learn to maintain good works, to meet urgent needs, that they may not be unfruitful" (Titus 3:14).

## Good People Experience Loss

After experiencing loss, good people will have life and prosperity restored to them. Dorcas's sickness and death happened for God's glory. The loss did happen, and those who loved her were deeply hurt as they wept for her. However, God received the glory because many believed in Him in response to the miraculous restoration of her life.

My story cannot possibly compare to Dorcas's experience of God's power. It is in her story that I find hope. She was a believer who showed her obedience to God's Word through her works and deeds, but sickness still invaded her body.

While we will all experience death in our bodies, it does not have the final say. God has given each of us the free will to choose where we will spend eternity.

I choose to believe that God will work through my personal tragedy for my good. With practical application of God's Word in my life, I am on a lifelong quest. This quest is to search the scriptures for the answers to even the biggest and hardest questions in life. I do not believe that God causes sickness or death, but in the midst of it, He tests our faith and trustworthiness.

## Can God Trust Us?

How many of us have blamed God at least once in our lives for something? This blame game might have been initiated because of the goldfish that died when you were a child. Perhaps, as adults, we blamed God when we experienced the loss of a loved one.

Turning away from God in the face of adversity is a sure sign that we do not trust Him. Running straight into His open arms is a sign of trust—one that He welcomes. When we turn to Him with expectancy and faith in His ability, He begins to move for our sakes.

## Can We Find God's Glory in Tragedy?

There is a reason you have survived. I am not implying that God gave you the pain, but He kept you here for a reason. You can now choose to use your pain as a catalyst to bring God glory. Anything that has died in your life can bring honor to God.

If you were sick, it didn't defeat you—you are still here. Praise Him and tell others of His amazing healing powers! If a loved one died, celebrate his or her life and memory. Tell others of this person's legacy and the things he or she achieved that brought God glory.

God is able to restore our joy. If we look closely enough, we will see that God is in the "furnace" with us just as He was with the Hebrew boys (see Daniel 3:19–30). He promises to never leave us and does not have a clause that states, "When times get tough, I am out of here." No, God does not lie. He will stay by your side.

If you can only muster up enough energy to say, "God, please help," know that He will. When I look back, I realize that I wrote those words, over and over, in my journal. He is faithful to move in your situation. He will calm the storm in your sea of tragedy. Just ask Him.

# Burn and Break

## Let Us Pray

Father God, thank You that I understand I am not beyond the reach of affliction. The affliction has happened to me, but I thank You that it will not overtake me. Thank You that because I love You, You will deliver me. Help me to not ask the question, "Why me?" but to cling to You and Your unfailing love!

Many are the afflictions of the righteous, but the Lord delivers him out of them all. (Psalm 34:19)

And we know that all things work together for good to those who love God, to those who are the called according to His purpose. (Romans 8:28)

# CHAPTER 2

# Do Not Try to Figure It Out!

## My Story

### November 8, 2012

Father God, today I received the doctors' report—hyperplasia, more surgery in the States, a breast specialist—a lot of words but no *real* answers. I choose to believe Your report—words written in red and inspired by You to us. By Your stripes, I *am* healed! I trust You, Lord. I see myself healed, restored, and delivered. Thank You, God, that the anointing destroys the yoke.

### November 19, 2012

Words like radiation, mastectomy, and biopsy have been spoken by the general surgeon here in Okinawa. God, I am believing you for complete healing and a testimony that will help others overcome.

## March 10, 2013

> God placed it on my heart last night that He is in
> control. Additionally, regarding the hair loss, He knows
> the number of hairs on my head. I know that God has
> His eyes on me. I will be careful to give God all the
> glory.

❋❋❋

> But it happened in those days that she became sick and
> died. When they had washed her, they laid her in an
> upper room. (Acts 9:37)

Dorcas's friends and family did not waste any time. They took action. Washing her body was a traditional gesture of preparation for burial. The immediate action of preparing her body was an example of how one must deal with the facts. We must take action. We cannot sit around waiting for an explanation. Life happens, and we respond with faith in action. Scripture does not record their thoughts on why she died but only their responses. They prepared her body for a miracle.

❋❋❋

This was not the time to conduct a Google research project. Statistics, studies, and too many medical terms and theories to name accompanied the reality of my diagnosis.

The enemy's attempt to lure me into his trap of "Why me?" occurred with enticing lightning-flash thoughts. Was it my diet, my work habits, my time management or lack thereof, my genetics, or a sin I had committed in the past that had manifested as cancer in my body? Should I begin comparing my symptoms to those found online? The answers were no, no, and no!

Without a point of reference to clarify these questions, the anxiety can push you into the open arms of another illness—depression. It is imperative that you do not become your own worst enemy by listening to the thoughts that will race through your mind. Condemnation will raise its ugly head and consume you with guilt, shame, and fault.

Immediately, I wanted to rationalize the situation, as this was my fourth time dealing with a breast cancer scare.In 2005, it was just a lump, so I had a lumpectomy (biopsy) that was too easy. The test results came in: it was benign (noncancerous)!

In June 2009, I again had a lumpectomy. The test results came in: We had a problem. They found DCIS (ductal carcinoma in situ, which in plain English meant that cancerous cells were present in the ducts of the breast tissue they sampled). We prayed. In July 2009, I had another lumpectomy. The test results came in: The margins (area surrounding the tissue sample) were clear. There was no cancer present. Victory was mine.

Then in 2012, the record scratched. You guessed it. There were more lumps. Honestly, my emotions were numbed, and the event quickly became surreal. I thought, *Not again. Not me. Not my life. Not my breast. Not now. Not ever.* Yet here I was again.

By this point in my life, I had acquired such a love for God's Word, I was full of His promises. I stopped my speeding and reckless train of thought and decided it was time for some practical application of God's Word. His Word consumes like a fire and breaks rocks into pieces like a hammer.

I thought over the facts and aligned them with God's truth. The difference for me between facts and truth is that facts are what I see and truth is God's Word, which corrects the vision of how I see those facts.

## What Will People Think?

I would like to mention that others may also try to figure out why bad things are happening in your life. In the next chapter, we will discuss the importance of what you are saying and how your words will define your thoughts and image.

The question, "What will people think?" enters the mind at puberty, in the early days of high school. The implications of this question can send you straight over the edge and into extreme living. This question can cause you to do unnecessary things because your actions may be based solely on what others *might* be thinking.

Yes, people will have their opinions of how this adversity could have happened to you and why you are now faced with a challenge, but the truth is, they really have no idea. Remember, that was what we talked about in the previous chapter. Others might analyze your past in an effort to determine what you have done to cause your fiery trial. In fact, this is not an uncommon practice as we see this very scenario take place in the scriptures.

In John 9:1–41, we learn of the blind man whose neighbors recounted him as a beggar instead of rejoicing with the once-blinded man and praising God for his healing. This clearly tells us that before the manifestation of your miracle is considered, what you have done in the past is subject to a trial, which is held in the minds of others. Was this an attempt to determine whether he qualified for such a miraculous healing? Possibly.

## What Does Jesus Say?

An interesting question in John 9 was presented to Jesus by the disciples. Yes, the *church people* asked Jesus if the man or his parents had sinned and had caused his blindness (see

John 9:1-2). I find this interesting because the disciples were in the physical presence of Jesus yet they too wrestled with the same underlying question, "Why do bad things happen to good people?" It was as if they were certain the blindness could not have just happened to a good person.

Jesus's response to the disciples is even more astonishing: "Neither this man nor his parents sinned but that the works of God should be revealed in him" (John 9:3). The Bible is timeless, and the stories therein have a way of exuding relevance thousands of years later.

God created humans. He completely understood the minds of humans and their ability to harbor such thoughts about others. I am grateful that He allows clarification in this area so we can close the door of reason as it pertains to what others say. So, let them (whoever that may be) talk, wonder, and try to figure it out while you rest in the assurance that it is for God's glory.

## We Will Not Always Understand What God Allows

As we quickly reflect, we see that Dorcas was full of good works, did charitable deeds for others, became sick, died, and was brought back from the dead. On the other hand, the blind man does not have a comparable description of his past. We only know that because he could not see, he begged from others. Yet they were healed and restored with the same love of God.

We do not get to choose who deserves the blessings, healing, or restoration of God or receive substantiated proof validating their qualifications for such. Neither should we attempt to qualify nor disqualify ourselves for the work that God is doing in our lives (after the tragedy), as He continues to work it out for His glory.

# Jesus Is the Same Yesterday, Today, and Forever!

Jesus performed so many miracles in His time of ministry on earth that John determines, "And there are also many other things that Jesus did, which if they were written one by one, I suppose that even the world itself could not contain the books that would be written" (John 21:25). This same Jesus is available to you today to perform a miracle in your situation. Jesus gave those that He healed a reason to live and not dwell on their former circumstances and qualifications.

## Wait on Him Even If He Seems Late

In John 11:1–44, there is a familiar survival story set in the days of old. We find Jesus's ministry in full swing as He walks on the earth with man, talking to man, performing miracles, teaching man and yet man had not prepared their hearts to receive all that Jesus was.

In its introduction, this story is about a man named Lazarus, who is sick and then dies. Lazarus's sisters were Mary and Martha. Lazarus was blessed that he had sisters who knew the Lord and called out to Him on his behalf. They sent word to Jesus that Lazarus was sick, in an effort to get Him to come and to heal their brother.

Jesus's immediate response upon hearing the news of Lazarus's sickness is recorded in John 11:4: "This sickness is not unto death, but for the glory of God, that the Son of God may be glorified through it." Mary and Martha knew that Jesus was able to heal Lazarus, but Jesus did not go to them right away as they had requested. In fact, the Bible teaches us that He delayed His departure by another two days.

We can only imagine that Mary and Martha questioned

Jesus's reasons for not immediately dropping everything and keeping Lazarus from death. Had they been among the crowds that witnessed Jesus's healing the multitudes? Had the two sisters seen Him bless and multiply the two fish and five loaves of bread, which fed over five thousand people? Why did He not rush over to their home, say a few words, and quickly heal Lazarus?

Jesus and His disciples went to Judea two days later. Lazarus had been dead four days upon their arrival. Jesus used the time of Lazarus's death to prove to the unbelievers that Lazarus was dead. While Mary and Martha grieved, they still believed Jesus had the power to bring Lazarus back from the dead. When He spoke to Martha, Jesus confirmed that Lazarus's death was for God's glory, "Did I not say to you that if you would believe you would see the glory of God?" (John 11:40).

Jesus told the people to roll away the stone and called Lazarus out of the tomb. He called him forth out of death's grip. He called him out of the bondage of the grave clothes. He called him out in front of the unbelievers and the doubters. He called him out in front of those who had been praying in order to reignite their faith in Him. He called him out to show His infinite power over death.

Survivor, hear His voice today. Get rid of those doubtful thoughts from your mind—never mind what others say. Silence the voice of reason, rationale, and regret in order to hear the voice of God. Do not entertain conversations with those who want to give their personal opinions of how and why it happened to you. It does not matter how you got here, how long it has been, or the good works you have completed (or not). Hear Jesus saying your name today and come forth. Once you hear the call, go! Do not look back or pause but just go!

# Burn and Break

## Let Us Pray

Father God, in all honesty, I would like to know all the details that will explain what is going on. Help me to understand that I should not try to figure this out but should place my trust in You. As I continue to seek You, You will direct my steps. Thank You, Lord, that as I trust You, You are protecting me like a shield.

Do not be wise in your own eyes; fear the Lord and depart from evil. It will be health to your flesh, and strength to your bones. (Proverbs 3:7–8)

As for God, His way is perfect; the word of the Lord is proven; He is a shield to all who trust in Him. (Psalm 18:30)

Trust in the Lord with all your heart, and lean not on your own understanding; in all your ways acknowledge Him, and He shall direct your paths. (Proverbs 3:5–6)

# CHAPTER 3

## Dear Survivor

# What Do You Have to Say about This?

### My Story

**November 6, 2012**

God, I'm not sure what You have planned for me, but I know that *it* is great, will bring You much glory, and is kingdom building. Whatever *it* is, I'm willing, Lord. Use me for Your glory! I love You, God. In the middle of the storm, I'm still going to lift my hands and say thank You! Thank You, God, for the peace that passes all understanding—Your peace.

**February 13, 2013**

God, thank You for Your peace, which You have given to me over the past couple of days. There is so much to consider. God, I thank You that I don't have to figure out any of this on my own. My faith, trust, and confidence are in You. You are the author and the finisher of my faith.

✧✧✧

Death and life are in the power of the tongue, and those who love it and indulge it will eat its fruit and bear the consequences of their words. (Proverbs 18:21 AMP)

One of the more interesting aspects of Dorcas's story is that there is no record of her dialogue. She does not say a word that we are left to reason with. We do not know her opinion of sudden death while doing the right thing. We do not know if she glimpsed heaven or had a conversation with the Lord as He perhaps told her, "Not yet." I will not add to this story because it is perfect as God inspired it to be written. I will take from her silence that I should be aware of my words in trying times.

> **Speaking before you think cannot produce any good thing.**

✧✧✧

Yes, it is really happening. The situation is real. You are not dreaming, and there is no amount of pinching that will wake you up from this moment. Now that you are looking in the face of adversity, what do you have to say? Do you understand the importance of what you say and how it will affect your thinking? According to the scripture, we can choose death or life with our words.

A survivor thinks about life more than death. A survivor will adjust his or her words in an effort to continue living. A survivor is a fighter who desires to live.

There is an incredible amount of power in confession. In

our day-to-day lives, contractual deals, covenants, oaths, and promises are created based solely on what comes out of our mouths! We speak without giving much thought to what we are saying. We don't realize the power of our words, especially when we are experiencing difficult seasons in our lives.

In the Bible, the book of Genesis paints the perfect picture of the power of words—creation. Speak life! This phrase is spoken frequently, and we should all take heed.

My definition of a survivor is one who survives circumstances that others do not survive and lives forever in heaven after receiving Christ as his or her personal Savior, *regardless* of earthly illnesses or afflictions of any kind. This is not only for breast cancer survivors. It is for every person who has struggled, has lost hope, has met defeat face-to-face, has not seen God directly fix his or her concern, immediately supply a need, or restore lost material things, has not received the promotion, or has not had a relationship restored.

God tells us to live, so think about living. The thing may have been lost, and the prayer may not have been answered favorably, but God is too sovereign to miss or to overlook the prayers of those who love and trust Him.

## Speaking Life for Eternity

You may ask, "What does speaking life look like?" God's Word provides an opportunity to secure eternal life through Jesus Christ. Romans 10:9–10 is the golden key to eternity. It says, "that if you confess with your mouth the Lord Jesus and believe in your heart that God has raised Him from the dead, you will be saved. For with the heart one believes unto righteousness, and with the mouth confession is made unto salvation." This scripture concludes that when we speak and believe, God gives us the ability to receive salvation. I believe that eternal life has always been on God's mind for humankind. It is vital to understand that when you accept Jesus Christ, it ensures that eternal life and surviving forever are available to you.

Likewise, I suggest that both the saved and the unsaved have an innate desire to survive in a peaceful eternity. I think this is apparent in society's willingness to spend money and time on superficial methods to lengthen life, as if living forever here on earth was possible. If this was not so, people would not succumb to advertisements for younger looking skin or surgeries that lift up and tuck away.

People purchase vacations in pursuit of a one- or two-week opportunity in paradise. They want the chance to lie in the sun and to enjoy the mesmerizing sound of the waves along white, sandy beaches near clear water. Seemingly, all of our spirits desire to be in a similar place—one of longevity and serenity.

A survivor has chosen life and will undoubtedly speak God's Word to live. A survivor will do whatever it takes to survive and to live. While here on earth, the survivor uses words that render surviving less strenuous and more enjoyable. The bigger picture is understanding that life on earth is temporary but that there is a forever we have the opportunity to obtain.

## Be Careful What You Say—You Just Might Get It

How many times have you heard someone who has an illness or disease take ownership of it? I have heard comments such as, "*My* arthritis is acting up," or, "*My* migraine is bad today," just to name a few. I am not suggesting that the tiny two-letter word *my* is the cause or the cure for the actual ailment, but it does make the situation personal. You should not take ownership of the things you do not want as if they belonged to you.

When we pray, we hope our words will be accepted by God exactly as we speak them: "God, heal me," "God, increase my wealth," "God, thank You for the new job," and on and on we speak. Using those same powerful words, we carelessly identify ourselves by our circumstances.

Please do not think I am suggesting I am Miss-Got-It-All-Together and the words in my journal are evidence of how I have always spoken. I have wrestled to accept my calling as a minister of the gospel. The conversation I had with God is an embarrassment to me today. It went something like this,

God, I will become a minister after I retire from the military. Furthermore, I do not have a testimony. I do not have this super interesting childhood story to tell that can persuade others to become saved. I have not experienced any truly significant or miraculous thing as an adult. The people will not want to hear me because I do not have any proof of who You are—You know, like those other preachers.

Yes, in my lack of understanding, this was my conversation with God. In short, I told God I did not have time to do what He was calling me to do. I did not have a raised-from-the-dead moment with Him to prove what He could do and who He was. I spoke to God as if I were a lawyer in a courtroom trying to prove my client's innocence.

The truth is, God did not need me to prove His ability to do anything on the earth. It had already been proven. I would like to add that this conversation took place about six months before I discovered the lumps in 2009. I was completely unaware that the breast cancer scare in 2005 was just the beginning of a long journey ahead.

What did I create with the words I spoke to God? Undeniably, I expressed the need for a miracle from Him in order to have a testimony of proof for others. I asked. He provided.

# Say It!

The importance of understanding that you are a survivor is essential in two parts. Firstly, you must know who you are. Secondly, others must know who you are. For example, the surgeon referred to the cancer in my body as "your cancer" while explaining the radical treatment that I would receive. I quickly told her that I did not want it and that it was not mine! The surgeon's words did not give me extra cancer, but I felt more powerful when I denied it was my property. My verbal expression to the doctor made it clear that I intended to survive without cancer.

Sometimes those around you need a clear picture of who you say you are. They may treat you differently, speak differently in your presence, and respect you for who you are. What are you telling others about yourself?

It is no easy task to find your identity when the part that defined you has been taken away. Regardless of whether the storm that you survived took your will, a part of your body, a loved one, a dream, or a marriage, you are still here. God's Word is the original and final authority for every believer's identity.

David found his identity and proclaimed to God in Psalm 139:14, "I will praise You, for I am fearfully and wonderfully made." David understood that God knew him and had created him perfectly in his mother's womb.

Has the situation consumed you in such a way that your words are like darts tossed aimlessly at a target—perhaps even at human targets? Does complaining about the situation temporarily soothe your pain? Have you lost your ability to speak positively during this challenging time?

You must believe in your heart and say that you are a survivor. Waste no words or emotions on blaming any person for this trial. Use your effort and emotion to find strength in God's Word. When you speak the Word and believe it, you will increase your faith and provide clarity in your situation. What you think of yourself is the key to your recovery. Picture yourself healed, restored, healthy, and even better than normal. Have confidence that you have survived as your words declare that you are a survivor.

## What Are You Looking At?

I recommend that you post God's promises around your bedroom and bathroom, especially on the mirror where you see your reflection the most. My niece Chandra visited me during my stay at the hospital. Because she understood my love for the Word and my faith in God, she decorated my room with Scriptures and positive affirmations. She literally went Crayola crazy all over that room. Colorful paper with her creative, handwritten effort to keep me focused adorned the bathroom mirror, bathroom door, and the door to my bedroom. Daily, I was forced to read those words, which removed fear and doubt from my mind.

I read healing scriptures and made them personal by thanking God that His healing was for me. I kept the word of God in my mouth, in front of my eyes, and hidden in my heart. I did not read the scriptures as a last resort but as an opportunity to see God perform His Word (see Isaiah 55:11), as He promised to all believers. I accepted the Word and the fact that healing and eternal life were promised to me. I realized that I would be healed on earth and in Heaven.

# The Praise Exchange

The prophet Isaiah provided a radical approach to painful situations as the Spirit of the Lord instructed him. In this timeless Scripture of great counsel, Isaiah says, "The garment of praise for the spirit of heaviness" (Isaiah 61:1–3). When we feel the heaviness of our circumstances in our hearts, there is an actual exchange when we begin to speak praises. Praise is a verbal communication with God that prohibits one from being consumed by grief.

Praises are the words that come out of your mouth and show adoration to God despite what is going on around you. During this process, God becomes your focus. There is good that comes from the fruit of our lips (see Proverbs 12:14). Fruit is a manifestation of the seed. Reading and hearing God's Word is the seed that produces fruit in our lives. What type of fruit is being produced by the things you put in front of your eyes and listen to?

Survivor, I challenge you throughout this journey to honor God with your words. You remember what your parents taught you long ago: Think before you speak! We must realize God has given us power through our words on earth. We can move mountains with our words if we only believe (see Matthew 17:20).

I now understand the power of God's Word and the power of the words I speak. I did not realize until I read the words in my journal that throughout my battle with cancer, I had spoken life. It came naturally to me because I had an established relationship with God and His Word.

## Praise Him Your Way

My mother is a PK (pastor's kid). She was raised in church even while at home. Not only was her father, my grandfather, a pastor but my grandmother was also an evangelist. The Word of God was planted in my mother, seed by seed.

My grandparents were of the Pentecostal (Holiness) faith. Trips to my grandfather's small country church were what defined the Holiness Church experience for me. The service included exuberant praise to God, dancing before the Lord, and pews and floorboards absorbing the shifting feet of those who had more praise than materials and more faith than results. They praised God in front of my gazing and often confused eyes.

I did not always understand why Sister "So-and-So" was lying on the floor because she has been slain in the Spirit. I did not understand the praise dancing, which looked like a jig, the shiny foreheads from the anointing oil, or the sermons that filled the air with the strength to change but without the profound eloquence of a seminary graduate. I never understood why my mother would throw open the doors and sometimes the windows of our home and tell the enemy that he had to go! Throwing open the sashes was not praise but my mother's way of maintaining her territory when she felt the interference of the enemy.

What I learned from those childhood experiences is that there is power in praise, actions, and faith when we believe that God is faithful to His Word. Do not allow anyone to dictate how you should or when to praise God. Of course, we will conduct ourselves decently and in order as scripture teaches us. Release yourself from the opinion of others. Refuse to be under the influence of other people's opinions. Speak what God has promised to you and according to His will for your life. Then watch Him do it.

# Burn and Break

## Let Us Pray

Father God, help me. My lips are made of flesh. Help me to speak words that will produce good fruit in my life. Help me to speak by faith what I am hoping for and not based on what I see. Thank You that as I speak Your Word over my situation and my life, I become empowered by Your Holy Spirit.

Death and life are in the power of the tongue, and those who love it will eat its fruit. (Proverbs 18:21)

Say to them, "As I live," says the Lord, "just as you have spoken in My hearing, so I will do to you." (Numbers 14:28)

# CHAPTER 4

# Stop and Focus!

## My Story

### February 21, 2013

> I am believing God for minimal to zero side effects.
> God, I thank You now for everyone that You have given
> me favor with: my oncologist, Dr. Perkins, for sticking
> his head in the room just to say hi and to ensure all was
> well; Carol, my nurse, for her patience and education;
> Melissa,[1] for her story of hope, and even her sharing
> her phone number. We all have unique stories. We must
> lean on God's understanding and not our own. Cancer
> will not defeat me. I will win with God!

During my first chemotherapy treatment, I was convinced that
I had won only because of my faith and trust in God.

❖❖❖

> And since Lydda was near Joppa, and the disciples had
> heard that Peter was there, they sent two men to him,
> imploring him not to delay in coming to them. (Acts 9:38)

The disciples did not send for the best physicians in their hometown of Joppa because they did not need a confirmation of Dorcas's death. Instead, they sent for Peter. The news of the paralytic, who had been bedridden for eight years and miraculously healed in Lydda, had traveled fast. As they paused to gather their thoughts, the Holy Spirit reassured them that Peter could also raise their dead. They stopped and focused on their desired outcome for their friend Dorcas. They wanted her healing. Swiftly, they went to Peter and requested that he come right away. This was faith in motion.

> It's all about timing to ensure purposeful reflection. Stopping is essential for proper focus.

❖❖❖

*Ready, set, go!* The call, which is used to initiate the start of any race, is made when the participants are in a stationary position. When life pushes you into a tailspin, you must *stop*. Once you are stopped, you have the opportunity to smooth back the pieces of hair that are flying in different directions, reapply your makeup, pull your shoulders back, raise your head up, and wait for God's signal to go.

While you are waiting, work on getting your mind in the right place. The mind controls each human's beliefs, actions, appearance, relationships, and the list goes on and on. The mind is the control tower that directs every area of our lives. In Romans 12:2, believers are instructed to be transformed by the renewal of our minds.

Transformation is a process, therefore, the mind is a constant work in progress. We must set our minds and focus on the things above (things of God) and not the things of this earth.

We must guard our minds if we want to control the type of thoughts we produce. What we put into our minds during good times is what will come out during difficult times and trials. If the golden nuggets of God's promises are not already in your mind, put them in immediately so you will be ready when calamity strikes. Daily deposits of God's Word, praising God, and hearing God's Word preached were methods that kept me peaceful when chaos appeared in my life. Those deposits are building blocks, which fortify the walls of your mind. Each block of mind renewal represents a guarantee of a return as needed.

## Focus on God's Promises

When I promise my children anything, they are quick to remember it, especially when it is a reward for good behavior. When I forget, suddenly they have memories that should empower them to become great scholars at the genius level. They remember each word verbatim and the place where I was standing, the outfit I was wearing, and the date and time I said it.

The same is true when I speak to God. I responded just as a little child does when I heard the surgeon's diagnosis and counsel: "Lord, You said …." I reminded Jesus of His promises to me. I am not sure where He was each time He had spoken those promises, but I found the exact place in His Word where He had said it.

God wants us to remind Him of His promises. I believe this is one of the ways He determines our level of faith. Do we really believe in the finished works of Jesus Christ and all that

He has made available to us? Faith is released when we speak to God about what He has said in His Word. This demonstration of faith shows God that we believe what He has said and that it will happen just as He has said. God is pleased with us when our faith is on display (see Hebrews 11:6).

## Focus on God's Presence

God's presence is too big to describe, too awesome to deny, and too powerful to underestimate. His presence confuses our sense of reasoning because we desire to see Him, to touch Him, and to hear His audible voice. After experiencing His presence, I can honestly say there is nothing like it. My best description is that God's presence can be felt in an untouchable place—the spirit or our inner selves. His presence is peace, comfort, hope, love, and joy all wrapped into one amazing moment.

I experience God's presence when I read the Bible, praise Him, worship in song during church services or at home, listen to gospel sermons, or have simple conversations with Him. I know that He is with me because the scripture says that He will never leave me nor forsake me (see Deuteronomy 31:6). Understanding His character and His love provides the assurance that in my time of trouble, He is with me. Acknowledging His presence was natural because I had become so familiar with Him.

## Focus on God's Future Plans for You

Only God knows the plan that He has for each of us (see Jeremiah 29:11). The plans for some are very apparent while others seem to have smaller yet significant roles in life. I knew that whatever my future held, while I was alive on earth I would glorify God by sharing my testimony with others. I had my mind set on a future where God was the center of my plans. In essence, my declaration included making a vow to God to tell others of His goodness toward me.

Focusing on a future after hearing the doctor's bad report gave me the will to live. I literally saw myself on the other side of the obstacle that had just been placed before me. The ability to put the future in the forefront of my mind was my way of encouraging myself in the Lord. I did not wait for someone to drag me into future hope while I kicked and screamed. I had discovered hope for my future before the trouble came.

## Focus on Trusting God

Trusting God is much easier to say than to do. When I am not trusting in God, I intuitively begin to try to do what only He can do.

God knew that we would attempt to work things out when we were troubled. In Psalm 46:10, He informs us, "Be still and know that I am God." God is telling us to stop and to recognize who He is. Trusting God is the best way to focus, as it enables me to access His power.

As I trust God, I release faith so I can believe His promises and that He holds my future. My trust in God is the foundation of my faith.

When your mind is set on who God is, it is also set on things above. This empowers the believer to look beyond what he or she can see here on the earth. While looking to God with childlike faith, optimism intensifies.

The excitement of how God is going to get me out of the problem is both exhilarating and mysterious. I knew He would do something amazing even though I only had hope and expectation and not always manifestation.

To know God is to admire the King of kings and the glory of His kingdom. When I begin to ponder who God is, I realize that He has all the power in His hands to immediately deliver me from my affliction or to walk me through it. God is faithful (see 1 Corinthians 1:9) and trustworthy.

Because of my trust in the name of God and His Son, Jesus Christ, I was able to put cancer under submission to His power. Once I put it under *submission*, it went into *remission*. I still had to go through the process, but cancer had already lost. I knew the power of the name of Jesus Christ because I had opened my heart to trust God. Jesus's name is above every name!

## Focus on Surrendering to God

It was necessary that I completely surrender to God. The events were unfolding so quickly and dramatically, I felt helpless without God's intervention. I wanted so desperately to fix my situation and to return to my husband, boys, and career in Okinawa, Japan, but it was out of my control. No method could fast-forward me through the pain, agony, and uncertainty.

Surrender is secondary to trust because you must trust God before you can surrender the problem to Him. God is not going to fight you to show you He can handle your situation. He just waits until the sweat is dripping from your brow and your back hurts, as does every muscle in your body. When you are completely exhausted from reading your self-help books and trusting the often-skewed advice of others, He will begin to work. When your hands are in the air waving the white flag, He will begin to work. When you speak to Him from your heart and tell Him that you surrender, He will begin to work.

## Cast All Your Cares on Him

Once I truly surrendered, I began to cast all of my cares on the Lord. The Bible is filled with promises, knowledge, and instruction. It is impossible not to love a God who invites you to throw all of your problems on Him. This is plainly written in 1 Peter 5:7, "Casting all your care upon Him, for He cares for you."

I experience a great release of anxiety when I cast my cares on God. I daily confess this scripture aloud during my morning devotion or quiet time with God. I give God every care that I have for that day. I thank Him in advance for working it out. My casting is verbal and intentional. The casting of my cares is like free-falling into the arms of a loving and able God.

Free-falling is what I imagine myself doing when I believe God beyond my own understanding. I have never skydived, but during my military training, I jumped from great heights with only a rope secured to my waist to prevent me from danger. During my military training, I also jumped from a diving board, which was terrifying, as I am not a great swimmer. I had to step off the edge of the diving board and into the pool. The fear was mind-boggling, but I naively believed that my drill instructors would not allow anything to happen to me. It is your choice as to whether it is like skydiving, repelling with a rope, or nosediving into a pool. Trust God the same way I entrusted my drill instructors with my life. Trust is a knowing and an unarticulated belief that God has got you. He does not like me better than He likes you. He will do the same thing for you if you believe and trust in Him.

# Burn and Break

## Let Us Pray

Father God, I thank You that when I stop, I rest. When I rest, You work! Thank You that You will keep me in perfect peace because I have stopped working and trying to fix what only You can do. I enter the rest You have promised me because I believe.

Set your mind on things above, not on things on the earth. (Colossians 3:2)

You will keep him in perfect peace, whose mind is stayed on You, because he trusts in You. (Isaiah 26:3)

There remains therefore a rest for the people of God. For he who has entered His rest has himself also ceased from his works as God did from His. (Hebrews 4:9–10)

# CHAPTER 5

# I'm Sorry for Your Loss

## My Story

**February 19, 2013**

Drinking the cup ... (Matthew 26: 39–42)

**February 20, 2013**

The day before the rest of my life changes forever, God is so amazing, and His peace is upon me. I know that I am safe in His arms. Thank You, Lord. No weapon formed against me shall prosper, and every tongue that rises against me shall be condemned. I am more than a conqueror!

**10:14 p.m.**

I am not scared, and I am not nervous. The peace I have comes from my amazing heavenly Father. Yea, thou I walk through the valley of the shadow of death I will fear no evil. Thank You, Holy Spirit, for Your presence inside me. Thank You that Your word abides in me. I am blessed and anointed for this cup I am about to drink.

Chemotherapy will assist with my healing, but I will not be consumed, overtaken, or beaten by the side effects. God, I thank You in advance as I set my mind on making it through every day, leaning not on my own understanding but trusting You and understanding that You know exactly where I am. You are not surprised or unaware.

I love You, God, for walking with me. Thank You for Your favor with the medical personnel. Thank You that they will be compassionate, knowledgeable, and willing to assist me. Thank You for sending forth Your angels to watch over me and to minister to me. *Lord, I need You now more than ever. God, help me!*

## March 6, 2013

The clumps of hair do not define me. I am a child of God. I am beautiful. I am the righteousness of God. I am not defeated. In Jesus's name, I overcome!

❖❖❖

Those who sow in tears shall reap in joy. He who continually goes forth weeping, bearing seed for sowing, shall doubtless come again with rejoicing, bringing his sheaves with him. (Psalm 126:5–6)

Please allow me to say that I am sorry for your loss. I apologize with the intent of aiding your healing process. When there is no one to say, "I am sorry," to you because

> **A loss is not losing. It is an opportunity to gain.**

your loss was not caused by an individual person whom you can hold accountable, it causes anger to arise. Have you noticed how much energy anger absorbs? Today, give yourself permission to turn anger into joy and to use that energy for the journey.

I immediately realized that my journey would require a tremendous amount of self-motivation. As I showered, nearly two weeks after my first chemotherapy treatment, clumps of my hair washed away with the water. The nurse had advised me that hair loss was a normal occurrence, however, actually experiencing the loss saddened me. God used the tears, which rolled down my cheeks in despair, as water that would cause me to rise to the surface of victory.

## Drinking the Cup

I use the phrase "drinking the cup" when I refer to the chemotherapy treatments I went through. I give all honor and respect to Jesus Christ for drinking the bitter cup of being crucified on the cross for all humanity. The loss that Jesus endured is incomparable; no human being will ever know how much He suffered. In Matthew 26, Jesus prayed earnestly for God to take the cup from Him and then said that it was not His will but God's will that should be done.

I had prayed, fasted, and believed God would take the cancer and its wretchedness from me. He did not do this, at least not the way I had thought it would happen. With the first day of chemotherapy approaching, I kept thinking of the treatment as my own personal bitter cup.

Ironically, when I visited my dad before going back to the hospital, he prayed for me. He held me in his arms as he began to pray over me and bless me. He asked the Lord to help me as I drank from this cup.

## Taking Control in the Chaos

I refused to lose myself in this process. I knew that my strength would come from God. Looking in the mirror, I saw a reflection of what cancer said I had become and not whom God said I was. In this surreal chaos, I took control of the situation. This control did not have the power to stop the chaos but to allow me to deal with things on my own terms.

I had already begun to research natural hair-care products for my African American locks. I spent hours following African American ladies on YouTube, who had found the best ways to nurture and style our hair type without chemicals or relaxers. My sister and I shopped at Target and Ross. At Target, I purchased hair-care products that I would not have a use for in the next several months at the earliest. At Ross, I bought beautiful spring dresses. I picked out the dress I would wear to my oldest son's high school graduation. I saw myself healed, healthy, and traveling thousands of miles by plane to witness one of the greatest accomplishments of my child's life.

I further took the power from the angry claws of cancer by visiting a hair stylist and having my thinning hair cut. Finally, I had my head shaved. My bald head made my youngest brother and I look like twins, which caused another moment of is this really happening to me? When I put on a pair of big earrings, a headscarf (or not), and lip gloss, I thought the look had fashion potential.

## Loss Does Not Define Us

As a parent, I taught my children from a young age that we always want to win, however, an occasional loss is as much a part of living as winning. It might be a defeat at a kickball game on the playground, the loss of a favorite marble, a friend walking away, the death of a loved one, or hair loss due to cancer treatment. The desire to win, to have, and to keep overtakes our ability to easily accept loss in any form.

In the midst of loss, it is difficult to see yourself as being whole, complete, or happy when losing someone or something. This was when I realized that my beauty was not only found in my hair. I had to allow my inner beauty to conceal the outer image.

You can't challenge loss by pretending it never happened but by acknowledging the loss. Mourning in some form or fashion is a typical response to loss. Surprisingly, when you realize your loss, the tears are no longer comforting. What can you do to move forward?

Logically, we try to replace things that we lose, but when what we have lost is authentic, there is no replacement. Committing to find a way to comfort your soul without being insensitive to yourself is detrimental. Substitution is not always the answer, but a plan for sustainment will bring about great peace. If you have to write it down and create a step-by-step plan, go for it. Whatever you need to do to get back up, do it!

## Not Defeated by Loss

Only you can decide how much more you are willing to sacrifice in your loss. Real talk: You have already faced an unbearable reality, and it has separated you from something that you had cherished, loved, wanted, and maybe even needed. Refusing to become defeated in this loss is your choice. Yes, you have the right to refuse defeat.

I personally felt my breast was something I needed. It made me woman. It was mine. It belonged only to me, just as my entire body did—and also to my husband. It created the perfect silhouette for my shirts and blouses to fit just right. It was part of me, but I could not do anything about the fact that it couldn't stay with me. Without it, I am still woman.

What I could control, I controlled. I could control my peace, joy, focus, and happiness. I am not sure if I ever properly mourned the loss of my breast because losing it meant that I would survive. The peace I found in knowing that my health would improve did not minimize the loss, but I used my faith to look beyond what I could see. In this vulnerable time in my life, I set my eyes and my focus on God and His Word. This was the only way that I could have had the power for sustainment in such difficulty.

## Embrace Your New Normal

A very dear friend, Miss Debra, who was also my fabulous hair stylist, once told me, "When getting a new haircut, you must be able to own it." When she said this, we both laughed uncontrollably because she always had a way with words. The phrase *owning it* means to embrace and walk with it while holding your head up high. In dealing with loss, it is not as simple as rocking a new haircut. If only it could be that simple.

Acceptance is acknowledging the loss and allowing yourself to feel and experience that separation without losing yourself. I daily face a constant reminder of my loss. Reconstructive surgery improved my silhouette, but I have had to accept that my body will never be the same. So I am asking you to do the same thing I have had to do.

I reached this place because of prayer and my relationship with God. One day, I did it. I turned around and looked cancer, mastectomy, chemotherapy, radiation, and reconstructive surgery square in the face and embraced it—I owned it. This was the new me. I was not the same but was still here. I did not die. Cancer did not kill me. I am still here today. Your tears may fall, but know that in time, you too will be able to embrace your new normal.

# Burn and Break

## Let Us Pray

Father God, thank You for the embrace of Your loving arms of comfort. Thank you that no situation I am currently facing or will face in the days to come has the power to separate me from You. Your love is beyond description, and your concern for me is breathtaking!

Blessed are those who mourn, for they shall be comforted. (Matthew 5:4)

For I am persuaded that neither death nor life, nor angels nor principalities nor powers, nor things present nor things to come, nor height nor depth, nor any other created thing, shall be able to separate us from the love of God which is in Christ Jesus our Lord. (Romans 8:38–39)

Yea, though I walk through the valley of the shadow of death, I will fear no evil; for You are with me; Your rod and Your staff, they comfort me. (Psalm 23:4)

# CHAPTER 6

# They Really Don't Know What to Say

## My Story

### November 19, 2012

Thank You, Lord, for those that are standing in the gap and praying for me. *Lord I love you more than ever!*

### February 16, 2013

It's a road trip to North Carolina! It is always refreshing to see my parents and to be at home. Heavy snow has fallen all day without accumulation. It's so beautiful! *God I thank you for this tranquil time & the peace* of love and familiarity. Let's take one day at a time with my hand in Your hand. Thank You for my complete healing. Lord, You are awesome.

❊❊❊

And all the widows stood by him weeping, showing the tunics and garments which Dorcas had made while she was with them. (Acts 9:39)

There is a mixture of faith, as we see the widows weeping and the disciples confidently believing for a miracle. Giving is such a rewarding experience for the giver and even more so for the one who receives. The widows were overwhelmed by the kind acts Dorcas had shown to them. They thought it was a great idea to show Peter the tunics and garments Dorcas had made—her handiwork. Their words did not come as easily. Showing how she had been a blessing was much easier.

> **The contents of the heart are revealed when emotions determine the conversation.**

✷✷✷

*They* or *them* are two words that are often abused. The words become the identity of unknown people. We have all heard someone say, "Well they said ..." and wondered who *they* were. For clarification, I am referring to those people who mean the most to you. Do not worry about what the other *they* have to say.

I have found that those who are closest to me, and whose lives I have touched just as they have touched mine, have stood with me through my toughest trials. I was blessed to have family and friends who said the right things to me during the time when I needed them most.

How did I avoid those awkward moments of conversation with others? I believe it was through prayer and unintentionally setting boundaries. The boundaries were, "You can say this to me, but you can never say that to me." There are conversations that people know I will not have with them. It is undoubtedly due to my personality. I'm somewhat guarded and private. This may not work for you, but you do not need to have step-by-step detailed conversations with everyone you know about what is going on in your life.

To genuinely comfort someone who is going through something, there *must* be a relationship. If you do not understand that person's personality, you are not going to effectively communicate with him or her in the midst of the storm. That relationship might also let you know that you cannot effectively communicate with that person, *especially* if he or she is in a storm. Without the relationship, trust does not exist. Without trust, no communication is valued.

## Even When They Say the Right Thing

We have all wanted to make things better for someone, and often before taking any other action, we try to console that person with our words. There are some things we should never say to hurting people. The intent may be good, but the delivery may not be received well. When there is a death, most people say, "If there is anything I can do, just let me know." In your mind you are probably thinking, *Can you resurrect the dead? If not, I don't think you can do anything to help me!*

When you are feeling emotions deeply because of loss and affliction, your emotions can switch without warning. You can move from sad, to confused, to angry, all within a matter of minutes or the length of a conversation.

While chatting with a mother who had tragically lost her child, I learned of a family member who told her, "Thank God you have other children." I am sure that family member probably had good intentions and wanted her to look on the bright side, but the genius revelation of "look at what you still have" can seem insensitive. It's important to understand the seasons of rejoicing and weeping as they pertain to verbal interaction with hurting people.

## Watch Your 'Tude

Your attitude will play a huge role in how others respond to you. Remember that fear and anxiety can drive you into dark places—places so dark that only God can find you. For Elijah the prophet, it was the wilderness and then a dark cave of despair, which he ran into because he feared the threats of the evil queen Jezebel (see 1 Kings 19). In God's confrontation with Elijah, He said to Elijah twice, "What are you doing here, Elijah?" (1 Kings 19:9, 13). God then reminded him that he was not alone and that He still had work for Elijah to complete.

Refuse to allow fear to create an atmosphere around you that others find detestable. As a survivor, when you feel alone, you are constantly in fight mode. This mode projects your willingness to live at all costs. Fight mode can drain those around you in such a way that they surrender to your tireless defensiveness. Ensure that your instinctive attitude to survive is projected as overcoming the thing that caused you to fight.

## Ask Them the Other *Big* Question

In December 2012, my sister Myriam, whom our family lovingly refers to as Cookie, dropped everything and left her life to be by my side as my nonmedical attendant during my hospital stay. Cookie, who is my oldest sibling, is eight years older than I am. She was the big sister, and as a young teenager, she could run the house in my parents' absence. As a child, she combed my hair, picked out my clothes, cooked my meals, and played a nurturing role in my adolescence.

When she agreed to leave her home in North Carolina to meet me in Maryland for my first hospital appointment, neither of us foresaw the extremes I would soon be faced with. The worst-case scenario we imagined was that she would be with me for the biopsy and then return home. Then I would go back to my life in Okinawa, Japan.

After receiving the biopsy results and hearing the ugly diagnosis, the first thing I wanted to know was if she believed God could heal me. Her wisdom, her maturity, and her belief in Christ were definitely good things to know about. I had to ask her the question that would help me trust her in my situation. I had to know what her level of faith was.

Did she believe like I believed? I believed God would heal me and spare my life. Cookie would be the one sitting in the surgical waiting rooms, accompanying me to treatments, and sleeping in the same room with me. Did she believe that God was still in the healing business? Can two walk together, unless they are agreed (see Amos 3:3)?

## Helping Others Help You

From the moment the first dark clouds rolled in and the rain started to fall, my family wanted to save me. More than anything else, they wanted to pull me into the shelter of their love and keep me from getting wet. They wanted to keep even the wind from blowing too forcefully through my hair. I know this because I saw it in my husband's eyes and felt it when he held me and told me that everything would be okay. Even though I knew he could not fix my physical ailment, I had to allow him to be there for me emotionally.

I had to remind myself that I needed other people and could not make it on my own if I closed everyone out. Some days I wanted to be strong and hold it together, and other days, I was glad to have the extra attention I received. Your loved ones need you to help them help you. They won't know what you need most unless you convey it to them. Your strength will come from God. Allowing others to be there for you will benefit both you and them.

Be careful not to burden anyone with the task to make it *all* better. Only God can give you the kind of peace and comfort your soul needs as an assurance that this too shall pass. Sure, other people can soothe your physical pain or stress with their assistance, but only God can calm your spirit. Once God calms your spirit with His peace and love, you are heading in the right direction.

# Burn and Break

## Let Us Pray

Father God, help my friends and loved ones to speak life in every situation. I thank You that those closest to me will seek Your face for understanding and wisdom. Allow words of wisdom and encouragement to flow faithfully from their mouths. Help me to help them be there for me!

Rejoice with those who rejoice, and weep with those who weep. (Romans 12:15)

A man who isolates himself seeks his own desire; he rages against all wise judgment. (Proverbs 18:1)

A man who has friends must himself be friendly, but there is a friend who sticks closer than a brother. (Proverbs 18:24)

Two are better than one, because they have a good reward for their labor. (Ecclesiastes 4:9–10)

# CHAPTER 7

# It's Okay to Not Be Okay

## My Story

### How Do I Look When I Am Going Through?

This question is playing over and over in my head.
If it's a sad or pitiful face, now that's something I dread.

I am a believer of God's time-tested and proven Word.
The preacher's last sermon was about faith ... yes, that's what
I heard.

Standing, in my understanding of faith, is to be noble and strong.
Shoulders back and head up, I must keep moving along.

No, today did not yet bring the answer to my prayer,
But I know that God has heard me, and I know that He is aware.

Are they looking at my face to see how I feel?
What do I look like? I just want to be real.

Reminding myself again and again,

With God, I never lose, and in the very end, the saints win!

Whispers of, "Just try to fix it," "*Don't wait any longer,*"
Now, that's not God's voice. Come on *now*, faith, I must be
stronger.

Shall I smile and laugh when I really want to cry?
No, that seems like a double standard, and why would I do that?
Please tell me, why?

It's important for me to keep my peace of mind.
I refuse to give in, allowing my soul to be filled with thoughts
of every kind.

Then it came to me as clear as a bell.
He let me live so His goodness I might tell!

So how do I look when I am going through?
I pray that my face is a reflection of God's love and His grace too!

**November 19, 2012**

> God, I resolve to allow Your will to be done so that You
> may receive the glory. Thank You, God, that I know
> and understand no weapon formed against me shall
> prosper. I understand now more than ever that there
> is a thin line between a *pity party* and *having a moment.*

❖❖❖

> Casting all your care upon Him, for He cares for you.
> (1 Peter 5:7)

Life does not ask our permission to change, but as each second passes, we are being led toward our destinies. Even the unpleasant details are part of a perfect plan to fulfill your purpose on earth. Despite your current situation or status, you can take control. Although you may feel a loss of control, you can give yourself permission to cry, scream, laugh, and not look like you have it all together. For some of you, this may be the first time you have seemed out of control, but trust me, it is okay.

Looking like we are out of control does not mean that we lose any sense of respect for our outward appearances. We should continue to dress ourselves nicely and to take

> **Even the smallest cares become too heavy to bear.**

pride in how we look. The control we once had while working the nine-to-five, bringing home the bacon, and being mommy, wifey, and perhaps even a good daughter may experience a shift. This shift may move you from being everything to everybody to needing somebody to be your everything.

At my place of worship, Bishop Terrence and First Lady Deloris Carr, at the onset of my survival quest, brought me into their pastoral office and consoled me with great spiritual advice. They assured me that it would be okay if I wanted to cry and allow myself to experience sadness. They both knew my personality. It was not one of a tough gal but one that worked very hard to look like she had it all together.

In their office, I allowed the walls that separated me from a vulnerable place to crumble. I cried but never rolled on the floor and screamed, "Why me, Lord, why me?" I am sure that I was probably thinking that. However, I learned from their great counsel that there was a monumental difference between having a pity party and having a moment. Here are my descriptions of both.

## Having a Moment

This is allowing yourself to process information that has altered the course of your life. This can be achieved through crying, screaming, or a combination of both. There is no set duration time, but this is a temporary state.

## Pity Party

This means wallowing in self-pity. You are unable to function as normal due to the amount of internal sorrow you feel for yourself. You are completely absorbed and controlled by the thought, *Why me?* This is a mentally unhealthy and continuous process.

## Ask for Prayer

When life knocked me off my feet, my immediate reaction was not one that I normally had in complicated situations. My normal attitude of "I got this" was not there. No, I did not feel that I had this. My awareness of God's healing power did not prevent me from initially feeling weak, powerless, and defeated. I prayed with a mind that was racing through every unfortunate scenario I could think of. My prayer was not yet purified with God's truth and peace. It was clouded by the facts.

My first cry for help happened when I phoned my husband after reaching my car in the hospital parking lot. He assured me that I would be okay and that everything would work out. He reminded me that God had brought me through this before. He did not want me to think the worst because it was too early to know what the test results would show. After God, my husband has always been my rock when the storms of life came.

My second cry for help happened when I called the first lady of the church. She was always so calm and collected. I knew she would demonstrate strength, humor, love, and faith, all at once. She did exactly that. First Lady Dee asked me if I had informed my husband. She verified this to ensure I was handling this situation properly by giving respect to my husband. Then she reminded me that God was in control and told me to go treat myself to my favorite Starbucks drink. She and I should own stock in Starbucks.

I shared the doctor's findings with people who understood the power of prayer. I desperately needed prayer warriors to pray for me. While my intercessors were bombarding the throne of grace on my behalf, I needed to move from the shock of possibly having cancer to finding my place beside them. It is important to know the character of the people who are praying for us. If they lack character, your request for prayer is pointless and will not be honored.

While imprisoned, Paul asked the Philippians to pray for him, believing their prayers and the Spirit of Christ would bring him deliverance (see Philippians 1:19). The church members in Philippi had supported Paul in his ministry and had demonstrated their love, which allowed him to trust them. The relationship showed their devoted action as they provided in his time of need. Paul knew that the Philippians could be relied on for prayer.

God had placed all the right people in my life for this time. In His all-knowing power, He had strategically allowed me to develop relationships for this season of uncertainty. These were relationships that had been nurtured over time—especially good times—and were now available to me in the bad times. They stood in the gap for me until I was able to join them.

## Enduring Hardship

In his exhortation to Timothy, Paul provided wisdom that is relevant today, "You therefore must endure hardship as a good soldier of Jesus Christ" (2 Timothy 2:3). Paul did not sugarcoat the possibility of hardship but said it would come.

Oftentimes, we have the false expectation that we are exempt from hardship as Christians. The confusion comes because of the distinct promise that God will *deliver us* from affliction in this present world. When we reach eternity, there will not be any hardships or afflictions.

Paul's instructions were simply put: *endure*. Yet enduring is not always easy. Merriam Webster's definition of *endure* presents three points:

1. To continue to exist in the same state or condition
2. To experience pain or suffering for a long time
3. To deal with or accept something unpleasant[2]

My career as a U.S. Marine entails a life as a *good soldier*. My success is found in the decision to persevere. It consisted of self-discipline, structure, and sacrifice.

Understanding authority is the foundation of a good soldier's success. Paul's analogy of a good soldier provides an example of the mind-set that is necessary to endure hardship.

## It Could Be Worse but Right Now Is Not So Great Either

Your right now cannot be minimized. Your circumstances do not improve by using the tactic of persuading yourself that it could be worse. It is extremely tough to place a value on this concept of worse. When life's journey has just taken you off the trail of the familiar and the comfortable, the measure of *worse* is inconceivable. All that you see, hear, and experience, in this moment, is clearly chaotic at best. In any really bad situation, *worse* is the best word to describe that moment.

One particularly gloomy day, the weather was cold, and the sky was gray, which added little hope to my already grim situation. As I walked from the hospital at Walter Reed National Medical Center back to my room at the Wounded Warrior Detachment residence, I began to self-motivate. I observed other Marines and service members in their worse, which included multiple amputations, traumatic brain injuries, and other illnesses. I began to compare my single, inconspicuous amputation to those around me. This self-motivation was an effort to avoid a pity party.

Just when I had convinced myself that I should not complain because it could be worse, I felt a scream inside of me. I wanted to yell at the top of my voice, "Yes, it could be worse, but right now is *not* so great!" This internal reaction would not have resolved anything; however, it would have allowed me to process my situation without condemning those feelings that things were not good. This single thought let me know my faith was still weak. Additionally, I could not find what I would need to make it through if I believed my situation was as it appeared. It was during this time that God increased my faith for the journey.

## His Grace Is Sufficient

God knew that we would have moments of weakness that only His strength could reinforce. My loss of control left me in a place of undeniable weakness. I could not heal myself, I could not remove the cancer, and I could not move the clock forward so that I would not have to endure the daily process of waiting for surgeries, treatments, and other medications. I desired for God's arms to carry me because I could feel the entire weight of my body with each step I took. It was too heavy for me to bear.

In His all-knowing power, God understood that I would need Him to guide me personally, as it pertained to receiving the chemotherapy treatment. My encounter with the oncologist went like this:

**February 7, 2013**

> Jesus's name is above every name—that includes cancer. My first impression of my oncologist's appointment with Dr. Perkins: He loves the Lord! The Scripture, "My grace is sufficient and made perfect in your weakness" (see 2 Corinthians 12:9) is embroidered, framed, and on his desk. Confirmation: This very scripture was put on my heart as I slept. God confirmed that He will not forsake me. My emotions were hardly contained as the doctor stated that chemotherapy was his recommendation.

Regardless of anything I had ever done in my past, God assured me, in that moment, that He would cover me with His grace. When we declare that we are not okay and acknowledge our need for God, we access His grace. God's grace was, in fact, enough. God assured me that I was going to be fine, even though I was not okay.

# Burn and Break

## Let Us Pray

Father God, the affliction is uncomfortable, but I thank You that Your grace is sufficient. Thank You that my eyes are open so that I can see beyond the pain to the purpose of it. Thank You that when I am not okay, You are. Thank You that You are with me in this moment and always.

Many are the afflictions of the righteous, But the Lord delivers him out of them all. (Psalm 34:19)

It is good for me that I have been afflicted, That I may learn Your statutes. (Psalm 119:71)

Even in laughter the heart may be in pain, and the end of joy may be grief. (Proverbs 14:13 AMP)

And He said to me, "My grace is sufficient for you, for My strength is made perfect in weakness." (2 Corinthians 12:9)

# CHAPTER 8

**Dear Survivor**

# God Hears and Sees You

## My Story

### February 13, 2013

God, I thank You that whether I retire early or transfer now, Ryan graduating in Japan or Virginia, and my level of treatment are carefully and divinely answered with Your love and grace. I completely surrender. *I cannot do this without you!* God, help me to stay in Your will. Order my steps that I may bring You the glory. Thank You for Your power at work inside me.

### February 22, 2013 (First Chemotherapy Treatment)

My hope is in Your Word. I won't complain. I have to give God glory, as I did not know what to expect. Tired but not worn.

### February 23, 2013

Please, God, help me and heal me. Bless Your name, God—the Author and Finisher of my faith. God, it is by Your grace and mercy that I wake up and face yet another day. Without any uncertainty, two things are true, and that is Your Word and promises. I know that Your promises are true and that You know the plans You have for my future. God, thank You for increasing my faith during this time.

I know that You will watch over Dayle and heal his back pain. I know that You will lead and guide Ryan and protect him from the enemy's snare. I know that You will protect, comfort, and lead Devin as well. I trust You, God.

## March 2, 2013

God, You are awesome. I praise You because of who You are. Today was unexpected—four hours in ER with a possible infection. Then there was no infection but more drugs.

Lord, please let the manifestation of Your healing appear in my body now. God, You are in control—not cancer. God, have Your way in me.

Thank You for the power of the Holy Spirit moving, working, and living in me. God, I know that everything could be worse. The most comforting fact is that You know where I am, and You know every need, every tear, and every pain. Thank You, God, that You have the answers.

❊❊❊

But Peter put them all out, and knelt down and prayed. (Acts 9:40)

Peter, an original disciple of Jesus Christ, followed His example. He had actually walked with Jesus and had witnessed His miraculous powers. In Mark 5:39–43, Peter witnessed Jesus raising a little girl from sleep (Jesus said she was not dead but was sleeping). In the same manner, Peter did not believe that Dorcas was dead but was sleeping. In the same way Jesus had sent those who were weeping out of the little girl's room, Peter did also. He did not want any distractions. He desired to get in the presence of God. Equipped with silence and faith, he believed that God saw Dorcas and would hear his prayer. Once Peter recreated the scene that Jesus had originally designed, he cried out to Him.

> **A prayer whispered or a quiet thought is loud enough for Him to hear.**

✿✿✿

I stood in the middle of a war zone as the enemy fired rounds from every direction. Simultaneously, the enemy whispered in my ear, "God does not hear your prayers, and He does not see your struggle!" The subtle tactics of the enemy will attempt to isolate you from the source of your strength—God. The constant threat of the shots being fired in my direction rendered me helpless. I found that the safest position was on my knees with my head bowed. It was then that a spiritual force field surrounded me, and I was no longer injured by the shots that so fiercely infiltrated my surroundings.

## How Do I Know that God Hears You?

I am certain that God hears you based on who He is. I make this declaration with confidence in God's Word and because He heard me. I am equipped with experience to make this declaration because of the time I spent waiting on Him without seeing any change in my situation. I make this declaration by the evidence of my healing and the answered prayers, which were too many to count. God will prove to you, just as he did to me, that He hears your prayers. God does not have *favorites*. If you love Him, He promises to answer when you call (see Psalm 91:15).

If your situation is anything like mine, this principle may be hard to accept. My family, career, and faith were severely impacted, and I desperately needed to know that God saw me. How do I know that God hears you? Because I did not lose my life, my mind, my family, or my faith. Yes, my career was over without an explanation from God. I am sure I will understand more as the journey continues. If not, that will be my first question when I meet Him in heaven. God will hear you, but you must seek Him, search Him out, and find Him.

## Finding God

God is invisible, yet His presence is visible each time we open our eyes. When we look in the mirror, we gaze upon the image of at least one of His masterpieces. When we look for God with our hearts, we will find Him while reading His Word. When we humble ourselves and pray, realizing our own weaknesses, we find Him. When we lift our hands in true worship to Him, we find Him. It only feels like He is not there when we fail to acknowledge His presence.

I immersed myself in things that allowed me to encounter the presence of God. I meditated and spoke scriptures that pertained to healing. I sang and listened to songs of praise and worship to God. I listened to His Word in church, on the computer, on television, or wherever it was being taught. My faith came because I continued to hear the Word of the Lord (see Romans 10:17). As my faith increased, I believed, more and more, that God was aware of my location, my situation, and my need for Him.

## Pray, Pray, Pray

I consider it a privilege to pray to God. God has the ability to hear our prayers whether we speak at the top of our voices or silently within ourselves. I used my journal to record my prayers, to communicate with God, and to hear my own voice. My circumstances were so loud, I often felt I could not hear myself think. Journaling allowed me to capture my prayers and the ability to reflect as God answered each prayer. Many of my journal entries clearly show that I was writing to God, and others appear to be a place where my pen and paper became friends that held my deepest secrets.

One of my very dear friends, Seneska, whom I refer to as my soul sistah, provided me with the journal I am using to create this book. She was one of those people I called on to pray for me when I had the first biopsy in 2012. The small hospital waiting room was overpopulated with my prayer warriors. I am sure she did not disturb the peace or draw attention to herself, but I know she was crying out to God silently as loud as she could!

I prayed when I did not feel like it and asked others to pray when I could not. I prayed when the pain literally put me on the floor, on my knees, and begging God for mercy. I prayed when I had a good day. I prayed when I had a bad day and everything looked chaotic and crazy. I prayed through tears. I prayed for my husband and my children. I prayed because prayer, along with my faith, was all that I had going for me.

## But God, I Am Already Going Through ...

Some would suggest that your luck is bad or that you had it coming (as we discussed previously). We must agree that luck has nothing to do with the unjustified events we all experience in life. Time after time during my battle with cancer, smaller tragedies appeared. Did God know that I was at my breaking point? Did He see the extreme circumstances in my life?

After cancer had intruded upon my life, my son Devin was hospitalized a few days before Christmas and two weeks after my departure from Okinawa. My son Ryan was in the fall semester of his senior year in high school and about to make the difficult transition of attending college in the United States. My husband, Dayle, was experiencing chronic back pain. As if the mastectomy was not tragic enough, my skin had an allergic reaction, which looked like it was an infection.

God heard me and saw me. He began to move in my favor. What I thought was the end of my life became a new beginning.

Survivor, believe that while tribulation may rock your boat, God still has the ability to command the waters and the winds to be still. Through Jesus Christ, you have that same power. Begin to pray and cry out to God. Rest in the assurance that God is not in heaven telling the angels that your problem is too big for Him. *You are not invisible to God!*

# Burn and Break

## Let Us Pray

Father God, thank You that You have heard my cry. Thank You that although I don't physically see You, I know that You physically see me. You are always near me. Thank You that You are aware of all hurt, pain, or sickness that is trying to overtake me. Thank You that my words have not fallen on deaf ears.

Now we know that God does not hear sinners; but if anyone is a worshipper of God and does His will, He hears Him. (John 9:31)

"Am I a God near at hand," says the Lord, "And not a God afar off? Can anyone hide himself in secret places, So I shall not see him?" says the Lord; "Do I not fill heaven and earth?" says the Lord. (Jeremiah 23:23-24)

Then you will call upon Me and go and pray to Me, and I will listen to you. And you will seek Me and find Me, when you search for Me with all your heart. I will be found by you, says the Lord. (Jeremiah 29:12-14)

Blessed be God, who has not turned away my prayer, nor His mercy from me! (Psalm 66:20)

# CHAPTER 9

# Look Up and Get Up!

### My Story

### No Fear, No Doubt

I know that God will bring me out from underneath life's concerns today.

It is with conviction, I will continue to say,

"No fear, no doubt!"

God didn't give me fear; instead He gave me power.

It's with that authority, I will boldly say in the early morning hour,

"No fear, no doubt!"

My feelings will not be based on what I see,

to avoid being that double-minded personality.

Simply trusting God means that I am blessed.

My past reflects that in His Word I have found complete rest.

"No fear, no doubt!"

God knew the end from the beginning.

The book of Revelation is all about the saints winning!

"No fear, no doubt!"

The rules of prayer have not changed: We have not because we didn't ask.

Just ask in Jesus's name.

"No fear, no doubt!"

The closed doors are okay to remain that way.

Keep pushing ahead, and we will see

the open doors if only we obey.

"No fear, no doubt!"

Rejoicing in this new day the Lord has made,

I can only do so because I prayed,

"No fear, no doubt!"

July 30, 2013

## February 25, 2013

I'm excited about today. My sleep was interrupted, but glory to God, I have no major pain in my body. Lord, I have a yet (continuous) praise this morning! Thank You that You are able and willing and have been time-tested and proven to have a record of victory. I can do all things I need to do in Christ this day. With God, all things are possible. God, I will not go on my own. You are still sitting on the throne. Defeat cannot grasp me, and failure is not an option.

## February 26, 2013

Today I stand proclaiming that God is great and greatly to be praised. I love You, Lord, and I magnify You. I exalt You. I am a woman of faith. I choose to believe, I choose to walk in victory, I choose to be happy despite the circumstances, and I choose to believe You for healing and guidance this day. If it had not been for the Lord, who was on my side, I would not be here! I trust You, God, and I know that I am blessed just because of that. Every situation in my life is under God's control.

✧✧✧

And turning to the body he said, "Tabitha, arise." And she opened her eyes, and when she saw Peter she sat up. (Acts 9:40)

Peter's power and confidence are profound. He commanded the sleeping circumstance before him to "arise." With this same fierce conviction, we should speak to those things in our lives that need to get up.

✧✧✧

One of the most courageous things I have ever accomplished was climbing the tallest mountain in Japan—Mount Fuji. On a clear morning commute to my temporary place of work, the snowcapped and brilliant mountains majestically towered in the sky. When the work assignment was completed, I, along with four young Marines, began our two-mile journey to the top. I was the senior Marine and made sure that my face showed boldness and confidence that we would make it to the top. Therefore, I looked up and began to climb.

> **Casting my cares on God silences the voice of fear, doubt, chaos, worry, and everything that would silence my peace.**

Metaphorically speaking, life has been like my journey up that mountain. Over the years, I have realized that the strangest thing happens when I arrive at a mountaintop in my life. I somehow transition to the bottom of the next mountain unaware. For a moment, I may find myself trying to gain my composure and asking, *What just happened? I thought everything was fine. I was just celebrating a victory on the mountaintop. Everything was going so smoothly, and all of a sudden, here I am looking up again.*

## Choices

There are so many choices to make in moments like these. How will I respond to *this* mountain? I can stand at the bottom looking at my feet, or I can begin to climb up it. Acknowledging God, crying out to Him in the midst of this transition, posturing ourselves, and looking up to Him are necessary. Meditation and prayer are the essential pieces of hiking gear that are necessary for this mountain. Then I can see and follow the trail up any mountain. So look up!

The next step, after crying out to Him in prayer, is to wait on God. The act of meditation sounds mystical. Meditation is a standard practice in different religions and is used for their own purposes. However, throughout Psalms, a proclamation of meditation is given. This simply means to remove all distractions and to focus on God and His Word. Like all sacred practices of Christianity, the enemy will try to pervert meditation if believers do not identify its importance.

## Do Not Fear Arriving at the Top

Once I arrived at the top of Mount Fuji, I was not looking forward to the hike back down. The pull of gravity coupled with the terrain proved to be painful and detrimental to my knees.

The same is true when bad news rudely sends you to the bottom of the mountain. But we must not be afraid of bad news. We must not live each day in fear of what *might* happen. The thought of success, peace, or happiness should not be clouded by the fear of *if*. Take a moment, breathe in deep, and enjoy the view on the mountaintop.

Signs had been posted alongside the mountain trail to warn tourists of loose rocks, which could cause them to fall to their deaths. Those warning signs disturbed the confidence I was determined to exude to those who climbed with me. I experienced that same feeling of unrest as I climbed the ladder of success in my career. In those moments of unrest, I still wanted everyone around me to believe I had it all together.

I used those feelings as a reminder to continue to move

forward with humility and that each step should be made carefully. In fact, the signs that warned that I could fall down the mountain kept me grounded on the mountain. The signs served as a reminder to step more gracefully. All warnings considered, I continued to move forward.

## Be Encouraged by the Successes of Others

Serving my country in Japan provided me with an eyewitness account of the longevity of the lives of our Asian brothers and sisters. On the streets of Okinawa, Japan, it is common to see elderly men and women riding bicycles and living very active lifestyles. So I was not surprised as I climbed to see men and women with gray hair descending from the mountaintop. Those that spoke English relayed the message that the top was, "Not too far." Let me tell you about the humility I experienced in that moment.

My body was secretly aching from the climb. I attributed it to my age, but my mind was set on reaching the top. While the happy, aged people of the Orient smiled, I grinned in agony knowing that I would make it to the top if I kept climbing.

The life experiences of others offers us hope in desperate times. I looked at those aged but wise climbers as a witness to my ability to accomplish the unthinkable. Looking back, I probably should have allowed others (other than Melissa— she talked, and I listened, but did not ask her any questions) to talk to me about their cancer experiences. The benefits of hearing more about how others had overcome would have been informative and comforting. I thank God for giving me His comfort even though I was unwilling to let others into my world.

# Getting Up!

Fear and doubt will plant your feet with the weight of cement blocks. It is impossible to get up and move with the paralysis of fear gripping you. The determining factor is believing that fear is bigger than God. Are you afraid of fear itself, or are you afraid of God? Being afraid of God is a reverential fear. It is knowing that God is the only true and living god. It is knowing that the beginning of wisdom is to fear God (see Proverbs 1:7).

Getting up is possible when looking to God becomes a priority. Getting up is realizing that the wisdom of God is essential for overcoming every stumbling block life rolls across your path.

Traditionally, universities are a place to obtain wisdom and represent a major stepping-stone to adult life. Institutions of higher learning are paid money to allow their professors to impart scholarly wisdom.

The wisdom that God freely gives will encourage you to also gain an understanding of His Word. The wisdom of God will guide you up the mountain of life which has been set before you.

# Burn and Break

## Let Us Pray

Father God, thank You that I will find my success in You. The strength that You provide me is greater than what I would have obtained on my own. Thank You, Lord, that You take me from strength to strength (mountaintop to mountaintop). Lord, I am going down on my knees and am looking up to You for help.

Give ear to my words, O Lord, consider my meditation. Give heed to the voice of my cry, my King and my God, for to You I will pray. My voice You shall hear in the morning, O Lord: In the morning I will direct it to You, and I will look up. (Psalm 5:1–3)

Blessed is the man whose strength is in You. Whose heart is set on pilgrimage. As they pass through the Valley of Baca, they make it a spring; the rain also covers it with pools. They go from strength to strength; each one appears before God in Zion. (Psalm 84:5–7)

He only is my rock and my salvation; He is my defense; I shall not be moved. In God is my salvation and my glory; the rock of my strength, and my refuge, is in God. (Psalm 62:6–7)

When doubts filled my mind, your comfort gave me renewed hope and cheer. (Psalm 94:19 NLT)

# CHAPTER 10

# Good Is Coming

## My Story

### February 24, 2013

My hope and expectation for healing is in God. Thank
You, God, that I understand that You know where I am.
Lord, I thank You for everything You've already done
for me and what You are going to do. I have overcome
by the blood of the Lamb and the word of my testimony.
I watched Bishop Cohen (streaming live). "The Church
of God *in* Christ" was his sermon title. It was a good
word. I will not try to figure out my today, *but I will trust
You God … Greater is coming!*

### April 4, 2013

God is love! Today, when someone asked what I learned
during this experience, I immediately stated "humility."
Next, I think the most obvious lesson for me has been to
be still and to let God fight my battles. God has made it
clear that I can do absolutely *nothing* without Him. I'm
learning to take time out for God and to listen. Spiritual

growth must be nurtured and constantly monitored. It is okay to stop and ask myself, *Do I feel closer to God?* Yes, God, You are always present, and I recognize that I must stop and check my relationship with You. Thank You, God, for loving me through my life and leading me by Your Holy Spirit into Your will. There are so many unanswered questions in the natural world regarding my life, my career, and my family becoming normal and in one house again, but, God, I am calling those things that are not as though they were. Thank You, God, for Your hand on my life and for keeping and carrying each one of my circumstances.

## May 10, 2013

I must change my view of the situation I am facing. As difficult as it was to be diagnosed with cancer, I choose to look at this affliction as a time to grow spiritually—physically healed and spiritually filled.

Then he gave her his hand and he lifted her up; and when he had called the saints and widows, he presented her alive. (Acts 9:41)

Peter called the saints and widows back into the room and confirmed that God was a healer. The good they witnessed was beyond all they could have imagined. Dorcas was alive. All of the tears dried up. The doubt was gone. The pain and suffering were finished, and the miracle had been

> Whatever happens today happens for me and not to me.

performed with astonishing results. When they had left the room, Dorcas had appeared to be dead. Upon returning to the room, she was alive. Can good come about so quickly and drastically for us when we pray and then expect to see a miracle?

❊❊❊

Is it possible that anything good can come from your most painful situation? Yes, it is possible. The suffering, loss, illness, or circumstance that put you into survival mode is going to be good for you. It is also going to be good for others. Good didn't prevent the disruption in your life but the result of the disruption is good. God's methods are unexplainable in this area. He has the power to work all things together for good if we love Him (see Romans 8:28).

## Now that God Has Your Attention

Let's discuss the moment I was shopping on Black Friday and a voice came over the intercom announcing, "Attention all shoppers!" Until then, I had never seen people in a store move as if they were in a life-and-death situation. That experience influenced me to never ever shop on any Black Friday again, where rude people urgently tried to find a bargain by any means necessary.

The psalmist in Psalm 119 writes that suffering caused him to pay attention to God's Word. The intensity of my suffering led me to open God's Word and to learn more about the Bread of Life (see John 6:35). God's Word became the only thing that would quench my soul's appetite for His intervention.

My suffering caused me to search God's Word, to desire communication with God, and to demonstrate the faith that was necessary to please God. My attention was focused on the things of God. I would have done anything to get God to heal me from cancer. I would have made a sacrifice, climbed a mountain on a forty-day fast, or given away all of my earthly belongings for one touch from Him. God's faithfulness did not require any of those sacrifices. Jesus Christ is the ultimate sacrifice for all who believe. I only needed to receive from Him, giving Him my full attention.

## Changing Your View

A change of view is necessary in order to move forward with a survivor mentality instead of a victim mentality. One very helpful and simple suggestion is to get rid of the question, "Why did it happen to me?" and to ponder "Why did I survive?" Your journey is not over. It has only been interrupted, paused, or rearranged.

I remind you, once again, you are a survivor. Why? Spiritual growth is a necessary aspect of the Christian life. The fertilizer used to grow believers spiritually is made up of the parts of life we consider to be waste. Just as natural fertilizers are used for growing towering trees and beautiful flowers, God uses the hard times of our lives to help our spiritual growth. During my suffering, I realized my need for God and my inability to do more than He could.

The strength of a person's soul is on full display when he or she goes through a trial. The soul is the mind, will, and emotions of a person. Desiring God's Word caused my mind to become stronger. My will was directed by God's instructions. My emotions were stabilized and dependent upon His promises. By His grace, I did not fall apart mentally. The moment-by-moment growth of my spirit and soul was the glue that held me together during my suffering.

## Suffering Is a Teacher

I will be the first to admit that a good book or a seminary class taught by a professor is my preferred method of learning to trust God's Word. If only life provided option A or B and door 1 or 2 when it pertains to suffering. I would have chosen the option of least resistance first to learn any lesson. The pleasure of choosing no suffering is unavailable in this present life but is an option for each of us later, in our heavenly home.

Cancer caused my suffering, and I didn't honor it. The good thing that came from it was that I gave God the glory for removing it.

Cancer taught me that God was a healer. I learned that God heard my cry. I learned that God could turn chaos into a celebration. I learned that my story inspired others. I learned that, with God, all things are possible. I learned that tears can be wiped away by God's hand. I learned that He truly gives beauty for ashes and a garment of praise for the spirit of heaviness (see Isaiah 61:3).

## Expecting Good!

Expectation is everything when you are in survival mode. What is your desired outcome? How do you see yourself living through and after this? Are you living or just getting by? The bottom line is that your expectation must be for something better.

I did not know that chemotherapy could have left me permanently bald. If my oncologist mentioned it, I didn't hear it. His voice must have became like the teacher in Charlie Brown cartoons, "Wah, wah, wah, wah, wah, wah, wah!" This medical fact had no power over my belief system. As I watched the videos on YouTube and purchased the hair products, I had high expectations that my locks of hair would return. In this case, what I did not know could not hurt me. That is why it is so important not to search for unnecessary facts concerning your situation but to search the Word of God for His truth.

# Burn and Break

## Let Us Pray

Father God, my expectation is that better is coming. My hope is in You and the promises of Your Word. Thank You that I know I will see goodness now—here on earth. Thank You, Lord, that my past will not cloud the vision of my future.

I would have lost heart, unless I had believed that I would see the goodness of the Lord in the land of the living. (Psalm 27:13)

Now may the God of hope fill you with all joy and peace in believing, that you may abound in hope by the power of the Holy Spirit. (Romans 15:13)

# CHAPTER 11

# It's a Process: Think about Living

## My Story

**March 17, 2013**

God, I thank You for the beginning of a new week. It is a new time for a life journey and *a journey of hope*. God, if I am not with You and am not for You, I am nothing. I thank You, God, for Your strength during this time. Thank You, God, for going ahead of me and fighting all of my battles.

I have had another treatment, and this time, I relaxed and focused on You with praise music, the Word, and the inspirational book, *The Pursuit of God*, by A. W. Tozer. God, I thank You for the peace that You gave me. I thank You that there will be no side effects, no allergic reactions, and no pain.

Although You have stated that I must go through, I am going through with You. I completely trust You. I will not worry. Your peace feels like the comfort of a warm blanket when the house is cold. It allows me to smile and to breathe with ease and to rest completely in You, surrendered.

## The Process

There is a process in every struggle that makes it unlike any other. Yes, each struggle has a beginning and an end. The variation is contained in the sequence of events within.

The struggle includes resistance and a lot of give-and-take. The way you respond determines the difference you will make.

The desire to give in as difficult seasons unfold will not allow you to see your dreams, so stand strong and be bold.

You may question why your struggle seems so much harder. Why does the distance of the road you've traveled seem so much farther?

The answer is simplicity and things you've overlooked. The struggle is not you, and you are not the struggle. We each have a distinct chapter in this book.

This book called life. The author wrote it with each of us in mind. He predetermined your life before the beginning of time.

Your struggle right now, as complex as it may seem, will catapult you to the next level beyond what you have dreamed.

November 22, 2013

I'm waiting on God and hoping in His Word.

 

***

Be anxious for nothing, but in everything by prayer and supplication, with thanksgiving, let your requests be made known to God; and the peace of God, which surpasses all understanding, will guard your hearts and minds through Christ Jesus. (Philippians 4:6-7)

Drip ... drip ... drip. The intravenous chemotherapy liquid traveled from the pouch, down the tube attached, to my chest port, and into my body. Drip ... drip ... drip. Is this truly the quickest method to receive chemotherapy? I had

> **Death will come without my assistance. Living happens on purpose.**

heard that some people received chemotherapy by ingesting pills. My oncologist had chosen the intravenous method for me. Drip ... drip ... drip. Who knew that this process would take hours to administer? Isn't there a needle you can fill with the chemotherapy liquid, inject it into my arm, and send me home? You know, like a flu shot or any other typical vaccine. No, this treatment was like watching water fall from a leaky faucet. Drip ... drip ... drip.

## Is It Over Yet?

In a crisis, one of the first things that enters the human mind is, When is this going to end?! Yes, that is the question with an exclamation point. It is a question coupled with emotions of anger, hopelessness, and sadness. It is never comforting to know that you are in a difficult season and the end is not in sight.

Why does it hurt so bad? Why do the tears flow as steadily as the intravenous drip of the chemotherapy into my body? They had ensured me that this slow process, consisting of a poisonous substance entering my body, would heal me.

It is during this process of not being able to get out that you become a survivor. Growth is cultivated in the toxicity of an illness, bad relationship, or other difficult circumstance. It is not apparent, and it does not feel as though anything good can come out of what you are experiencing, but after the process is complete, you will be stronger.

## Pray and Praise God!

Pray and praise God! Pray some more and praise God louder. After you have prayed and praised loudly, repeat the process with an even greater diligence. Over and over, you create an atmosphere that counters what you are going through.

The power in your self-created process is that you begin to focus on God and His strength and not on your own. The ability to make it through your struggle never depended upon you and your strength but your willingness to accept the strength of our loving God. Decide that while you cannot control the thing that you are going through, you do have control over the way you react to it.

## Journey to Hope

Where is hope when you have pain, defeat, and struggles to deal with? What is hope when you are looking at hopelessness? The struggle appears to destroy the hope one person possesses. This is not true. Grab your walking stick, lace up your best athletic shoes, and put on your headphones. Yes, that praise music is going to allow you to set your internal GPS destination to hope.

Hope is not necessarily a place but a desire for what you cannot see. It is closely intertwined with faith. Faith becomes the substance of things hoped for (see Hebrews 11:1). You cannot have faith without hope nor hope without faith. Hope becomes a choice between defeat and victory. What are you choosing? This decision is entirely up to you.

## Beauty in the Process

In this process of struggle, which has an ugly appearance, feel, smell, sound, and taste, where is the beauty? Nothing in your physical situation will allow you to look past its ugliness. Get out of your emotions and, in essence, out of your own way. Now activate your hope and faith without logically considering your circumstances. There is beauty in this chaotic situation, which has shown you no mercy. Do not wait in the halls of the courthouse while you struggle for mercy. We serve a God who gives us new mercy every day (see Lamentations 3:22–23).

The beauty you find is sure to be different from the next person's. Unfortunately, my life is only one of the millions that has been disrupted by cancer, but the beauty that I have from the struggle is individually and personally my own. My story has left a beautiful scar, which will allow only me, through the lens of my experience, to write this book. Yes, many choose to write stories about their battles with cancer, but the similarities will not create an identical story. The beauty that you will find in your struggle becomes your own.

## Think about Living

If you are struggling with the thought of death, think about living. If you are struggling with the thought of poverty, think about living with prosperity. If you are consumed with the thoughts of guilt and condemnation from your past, think about living in freedom. If you are struggling with what another person did to you, think about living without his or her control over you. You do not have to settle for defeat. Remember that is your choice.

In survivor mode, you do not want to think about dying. A survivor wants to live, breathe, and move after the struggle. A survivor understands that death will occur to every person, but in the meantime, that person will think about living. Praising God in song, reading His Word, or just saying words of adoration to Him, always causes me to think about living. The peace and joy found in His presence is available to you. Praise becomes surrender, and surrender becomes rest. When we enter into His rest, God brings the struggle to an end.

# Burn and Break

## Let Us Pray

Father God, through the process of my current situation, I realize that my faith is necessary. Thank You for increasing my faith and keeping me focused on living today. With Your mercies, I am able to face today. Thank You, Lord, that because of Your faithfulness, I will see those things that I am hoping for.

Now faith is the substance of things hoped for, the evidence of things not seen. (Hebrews 11:1)

To console those who mourn in Zion, To give them beauty for ashes, The oil of joy for mourning, The garment of praise for the spirit of heaviness; That they may be called trees of righteousness, The planting of the Lord, that He may be glorified. (Isaiah 61:3)

Through the Lord's mercies we are not consumed, Because His compassions fail not. They are new every morning; Great is Your faithfulness. (Lamentations 3:22–23)

# CHAPTER 12

# Consider What He Has Done and Then Tell Someone

## My Story

### January 31, 2013

I will walk out of this time of my life into a life that is filled with glorifying God, telling my testimony, and sharing His goodness.

### February 17, 2013

This evening, I looked in a bathroom mirror in the house I grew up in and thought about my reflection. This was a reflection of my past and present. Gone was the little girl, who had doubt and was uncertain of her mysterious future. Now standing and looking back at me was the grown woman I had become, who had a new perspective on life and understood that the future is held in my great God's hands.

This reflection was not concerned with what I was wearing, whether or not I was cool, if my hairstyle was looking okay, or whether I was good enough. Confidently, I concluded that I loved me and that growing into the woman I had become had been quite the journey.

I am grateful for every day, every rocky place, every dry place, every success, every smile and, I must include, every tear. I exist for the purpose in which God created me. I am walking the road of my destiny, which was written before I took my first breath. God, I thank You for keeping me, and I pray that I will run with the vision You have given me for my life with You.

## September 9, 2013

There is so much to be grateful for, yet my humanistic side can always find something to disrupt the peace and awesome testimony I have, which can overcome major obstacles. Life is such a beautiful experience as long as I keep my mind from becoming a trash collection center. I must constantly be refreshed and look back at where He has brought me from.

*\*\**

And it became known throughout all Joppa, and many believed on the Lord. (Acts 9:42)

The beauty of God is remembered as we consider what He has done in the lives of others and our own. The saints and widows witnessed

> **When I tell my story, I take back control.**

a miracle because Peter obediently answered when they called upon him. He interceded on behalf of another disciple with steadfast and immovable faith as he considered what the Lord had done before.

Dorcas's situation did not look impossible to Peter. Peter's faith and the manifestation of God's healing power caused many to believe in the Lord. This is an excellent, true story, which shows the importance of remembrance and sharing the marvelous works of God.

❖❖❖

We must accept the past and embrace the present in order to move into the future. Every detail of life, both past and present, moves each person closer to his or her destiny. For example, a basketball player who is chosen as the most valuable player would not achieve such an honor without the coach evaluating the past and present performance of the player. Without the past, which is obviously great in this situation, there would be no foundation for the assessment of performance. Remembering the things that God has done in your life will sharpen your focus on what He can do in your future.

When I consider all the works God has performed in my life, my heart flutters with excitement. In hindsight, there were many times in my life when God's intervention prevailed. A few of them include saving me from harm, healing me, delivering me, removing temptations, opening doors, closing doors (yes, I do thank Him for the closed doors), and always supplying my needs. God is constantly working things out in our lives even when we cannot see, feel, touch, or hear Him do it.

When a mother sees a child's handprints on an otherwise spotless window, freshly painted wall, or a polished refrigerator door, her urge is to immediately scold the child. I have learned that as my children have grown up (now a young adult and a middle schooler), I have sorely missed those handprints.

Similarly, God's handprints completely cover each day of our lives. Unlike the handprints of our children, which appear immediately and right after cleaning, God's handprints can only be seen when we purposely meditate on our lives.

You may ask yourself, *Why should I think about what He has done? I need Him to do something now!* The benefit of thinking about what He has done will help you build trust (knowing that He will), build confidence (knowing that He is able), and build expectation (knowing that you can look forward to His intervention).

## Knowing That He Will Because He Is Able

I have previously discussed trusting in God. It is such an essential part of my relationship with Him. Surviving adversity is not possible without trust and keeping trust as the scope through which I view every situation. I can easily compare it to a sharpshooter looking through the lens of the weapon's scope. If the shooter looks away from the lens and directly at the target, it will appear blurry, and the bullet will never reach its intended target. Trust guides the trajectory of our faith. When we believe that God is able, it is a guaranteed hit—a bull's-eye.

I have spent many nerve-racking moments on the weapons' range as a Marine. Throughout my career, it was always a huge challenge for me to qualify with the rifle and the pistol. The training always began in the early morning hours. Marines are well-known for their resourcefulness. We never waste sunlight when training is involved. The night before my training would bring on an unsettled stomach and the big question, What happens if I fail my marksmanship qualifications?

Over the years, weapons marksmanship became easier because of my past experiences. My confidence increased as I considered the previous year's qualification. A quick glance at my training record revealed a list of my scores, and a peek at my shiny medal earned by my capabilities soon outweighed my concern. It was my track record that overcame my doubt and nervous stomach. The work of the Lord, in His written Word and in my life, allows me to confidently expect Him to perfect everything that concerns me.

## Constant Refreshing

The Bible is filled with the great works of God and His Son, Jesus Christ. When I do not spend time in His Word, I feel parched and spiritually dry. A feeling of refreshment is produced by the constant renewal of my mind in the Word. Yes, I'm talking about the power of the Word again!

A gym workout that leaves you sweaty carries the reward of a hot shower, which is priceless. The grime of sadness, sickness, bad news, or maltreatment from others can leave stains on our hearts that require cleansing. If only pain could be removed by simply scrubbing with a bar of soap.

Time spent daily in the Word of God allowed me to remove the stain of cancer from my mind. The more I read about the character of God, the more I realized how much He had demonstrated who He was to me.

If you do not believe you can enjoy this same refreshment, I challenge you to journal the differences that occur in your day when you read His Word and when you don't. This is not a double dare. I do make a disclaimer that I am not responsible for your day without Him. Taking me at my word as it pertains to the benefits of renewing your mind is less painful than accepting the challenge.

# Did You Give Him Your Word?

How many times have you been in a back-against-the-wall situation and have pleaded with God? I personally recall on many occasions saying, "Lord, if you just get me out of this I will ..." I am confident that a lot of you are nodding your head right now in agreement. Perhaps, some of you are laughing aloud as you think of what you have said you would do if God showed mercy.

Lamentations 3:22–23 teaches us that we are not consumed because of His mercy. Our cry to God to give us something brand-new every day is normal.

As I journaled, I wrote to God several times that I would tell of His glory. I gave Him my word, over and over. A reality check came later in my personal study of Psalm 66:13-14. I had made a vow to the Lord when I had been in trouble. A vow spoken is better not said if it is not going to be fulfilled. I had not only said it but written it. In our world system where written contracts are nonnegotiable, how much more is this true when we give our word to our Creator? Whatever you promised to God in the midst of your trouble, *do it*!

# Your Story Is Significant

My story is captured in the journal entries I wrote as I sorted through my thoughts and emotions in the midst of my battle with cancer. My story may not be the worst one you have ever heard, but it is mine. My story may not measure up to that of other cancer patients, but it is mine. My story cannot be compared with others but should be used to encourage those who have a divine appointment with destiny. My story is part of me. My story is like my DNA: it identifies what I am, where I came from, why I am here, and to whom I belong.

Your story is valuable, and you did not experience it in vain. The entire world should hear your story so that those who need to hear it will have the opportunity. Think about the things God has done or is currently doing in your life and begin to strategize how your story can be used for the good of others. You can start by telling the cashier at the grocery store. Maybe your hairdresser, your manicurist, your neighbor, the person in line behind you, or the friend who appears to have it all together need you to tell your story. Somebody needs to hear what you may consider to be insignificant. Your story has the power to change someone's life.

## If You Do Not Tell It, Someone Else Will!

God will not wait on you to decide if you will tell what He has done. He will give another person the wisdom to express what He has given to you. My husband can witness to this truth in my life: Since 2008, God has revealed and confirmed to me that I would become an author. Even this final chapter, which I began over two years ago, was recently the main idea of a Christian broadcast. Many book titles I have received inspirationally have been used by other people. One book title even became a Tyler Perry stage play. Even though God has supplied me with creative power, He is not going to beg me to use it.

In other words, someone else can tell his or her story to a world in need, and it can be as powerful as your story would have been. Keeping in mind that your story is significant, please recognize that God will get His message of goodness and redemption to this world whether you help or not. It is not about you or me. Yes, it was our pain, loss, suffering, or circumstance but all for His glory. If He allowed you to go through it, use it to bless and encourage someone else. Now tell it!

## Go Tell Your Story

A song verse I have heard since I was a child is ringing in my heart right now. I have heard this song performed in different ways and by many choirs and singers, but here is how it goes: "I get joy when I think about what He's done for me [repeat]! You don't know like I know what He's done for me [repeat]**). You can't tell it, let me tell it, what He has done for me**! [repeat]."

With an angelic voice, someone, whom God had moved powerfully in, ministered with this song, which always guaranteed to exceed the three-to-five-minute time window expected of any Sunday morning hymn. Over and over with passion and conviction, the lyrics would sail through the air, piercing the hearts and minds of all. A testament of what God has done for anyone should only be compared or shared to bring God glory.

It is not a contest or a big-fish story. Your story is as unique as your fingerprint. Your story can change the course of a life that needs just one more story, one more word, or one more reality that God is in control. Let nothing stop you from telling others how great God is and how, even in adversity, He never left your side. I challenge you to start today. There is freedom in telling your story, your way, for His glory. Yes, it happened, and no, it probably does not seem fair, but take control. What can you do now? Tell someone your story, give God the glory, and watch, wait, and witness as He begins to bless you for your obedience.

# Burn and Break

## Let Us Pray

Father God, thank You that I will courageously tell all that You have done. Lord, I thank You that I will share the story of Your works in my life with those who need to hear it most. Thank You that others will have faith and believe that You will be with them just as You are with me. Thank You, Lord, that each time I tell my story, You receive the glory!

I will also meditate on all Your work, and talk of Your deeds. (Psalm 77:12)

Now the Lord is the Spirit; and where the Spirit of the Lord is, there is liberty. (2 Corinthians 3:17)

I will sing of the mercies of the Lord forever; with my mouth will I make known Your faithfulness to all generations. (Psalm 89:1)

# FINAL WORD

# Jesus Is the Cure!

**November 4, 2013**

Wow! Amazing grace! I know that God healed me from cancer not once, but twice, and I know that He is a healer. A lightbulb just came on as bright as a lightning flash as the thought passed through my mind, bypassing all scientific studies and research. Lord, I feel that you are looking at your people and thinking, *Don't waste any more money. Don't run one more race. Here I am. It's Me, God the Father, Jehovah Rapha, the One who heals.*

The cure to my ailment abides in me.

Forgive me, Lord, for almost overlooking Thee.

You waited so quietly as I listened to the facts of the world, nearly neglecting the truth of Jesus Christ, which I learned as a small girl.

# NOTES

1   Melissa shared her story with me while we were in the same room with the nurse. Melissa was beginning treatment for the cancer, which had attacked her again. She talked without breathing convincingly, and I am sure she quietly reassured herself. As sweet as she was in that moment, I never used her phone number. It was still too new, too fresh, and too soon to expose my wound to others.

2   *http://www.merriam-webster.com.*

Printed in the United States
By Bookmasters